Teeth, Hair & Tits

Teeth, Hair & Tits

A Story of Resilience and PTSD

by
Kim Price

This book is dedicated to my children,
whose love, trust and honesty has
kept me true to myself.

'I hope, to know that honesty is the first chapter in the book of wisdom.'

From a letter written by Thomas Jefferson to Nathaniel Macon Monticello, January 12, 1819

Setting the Tone (Preface)

This book is for those trapped by terrible memories. It is a book for people who are hurting and struggling with their mental well-being. It is a book for people who worry they may be going mad or having a nervous breakdown, for those who want to scream or run away or hide. You can't meditate or exercise bad stuff away; you have to face it, feel it and process it. I wrote this book to help people do just that. Understanding our feelings, understanding our reactions and responses to life's constant challenges helps us understand what is going on in our heads. When we understand that, we stand a chance of keeping a loose hold on the reigns of our life. Understanding helps us appreciate why we may be living in survival mode rather than the more rewarding thriving mode. Sometimes, just surviving is good enough. It was like that for me for a time. Just keeping going was an achievement. But there came a time when I was crying inside and I had to stop, understand what was happening to me, face it, and unfreeze so I could begin to heal and live again.

We hear so much encouraging conversation today about 'asking for help' for mental health issues. Asking for help is a critical step; you can't get free of mental illness alone. You can't think or breath problems away, you can't just forget: it requires professional help. In my head I hear the sayings, 'If you don't ask then you don't get', 'One can't read minds', 'Better out than in', 'A problem shared is a problem halved' and 'Keeping it bottled up does no good'. These sayings are well intended and are based on common sense, and for those of us on the extroverted end of the personality spectrum, this is advice we often take; we talk, we open up, we get it out. In doing so we often feel much better. But I know many people who don't feel the need to talk to solve problems, and that's fine most of the time. I have lived with, and loved, family members that can't put into words what they want to say, problem or no problem, and at times that can be frustrating for all concerned. But when you feel bad and the negative feelings start to impact on your well-being and ability to function, I believe not being able to talk is a handicap. Not being able to define, describe or relate mental issues, limits and often prevents people from getting the help they need and deserve. When you feel bad inside, even the most extrovert of us can clam up, retreat, and close off the communications channels. I am by nature an extrovert, but even I struggled to verbalise the feelings that came with PTSD. For a long time I was hiding the pain, I was ashamed of my feelings, I was scared of my emotions; and worst of all,

I tried to dismiss them, ignore them, and it was this that led to problems beyond PTSD. Bottling up led to additional problems in my gut and mouth. When I did manage to talk, I got the right diagnosis, the help I needed and in time, with much work, my mojo back. To get help for mental illness, someone has to understand you and nine times out of ten this is achieved by someone listening. For that to happen someone else has to talk. I wrote this book first and foremost, to heal myself. I published this book to give words to those struggling to talk, to those seeking help for what they think may be PTSD in themselves or a loved one, and to give encouragement to those already on the path to getting free of PTSD. My journey was painful, exhausting, disturbing, alarming and bloody hard work. The path was untrodden and bumpy; worst of all, I had no idea how long the journey would take. But I did not journey alone; my family, friends, therapist and GP travelled with me. The good news is that PTSD can be successfully treated, even when it develops many years after a traumatic event. I bear witness to that fact. Believe me and read on.

When I first decided to publish my scribbles I had a lot of things to consider, the first being was it a good idea? At the time I decided to publish I was still nowhere near free of PTSD. Was publishing fair on my family? Whilst separated from my husband, I was not divorced.

The Covid pandemic was killing thousands a day in the UK alone. These were valid enough reasons to reconsider, and put the book on the back burner. The writing had not been a waste of time; it had helped me come unstuck from the disabling emotional glue of PTSD. So that was good enough, surely? But then I began to hear of, and see, the fear and anxiety in others. Mental health and PTSD were all over the news, internet and discussion forums. I knew myself that there were very few books written specifically about living with PTSD. The few books I did locate were mainly written by veterans within a military context, related to a US setting or written by health professionals or established authors. When I was suffering the worst of my symptoms with PTSD the most helpful, digestible and relatable books that I found covered anxiety and depression, written by Matt Haig. But anxiety and depression were only part of the disabling aspects of my PTSD. I realised that through my own experiences I might be able to help others. It was as I was exploring publishing options, I came across a blog by Paula Mosher Wallace in which she talked about 'writing in pain rather than writhing in pain,' and her words prompted me to revise my scribbles from a place of hurting and healing, to one of helping.

I want to give people who are suffering with mental illness helping words. Words are essential to human communication; my story may provide someone with the words they are looking for; words of honesty, comfort, solidarity and humour. I want to be the catalyst for action, I want to inspire people to get help, and not accept living with the disabling symptoms associated with PTSD or other related mental health conditions. Along the way, I hope not to harm, confuse, offend, belittle, or bore readers.

I know first-hand (having lived with two introverted, dyslexic people) how frustrating it is not to be able to find the words to say how you feel, or what you think or mean. It's painful for all parties involved. Talking is not everything; there are other ways we humans show our emotions, with tears, laughter and body language. Sometimes we don't need words when we can say much and feel much with music or pictures. Napoleon Bonaparte's quote 'Un bon croquis vaut mieux qu'un long discours' translates as 'A good sketch is better than a long speech'. Nevertheless, conversation, dialogue, language and narrative are important vehicles for understanding each other and building relationships. When someone close to me used to say, 'you know what I mean', I wanted to scream. I'd no idea what was meant. I tried to understand in the absence of words but so often I was way off and we got nowhere.

"Words are not thoughts, just as bricks are not homes. But houses are made with bricks. If you have less bricks, you will make a small house. So, the more words you have, the clearer your thoughts and the more clearly you can covey them.........

You know what I mean? is running out of words"

Translation from an online Ted Talk, *The Gift of Word* by Javed Akhtar (poet & screenwriter)

My story does not stand still, as life goes on my thoughts ramble with me and I thank my genes for my gift of the gab; this book is my mansion.

Contents

Why Write?

I live by the motto: 'it's not what happens to you that matters, it's how you tell the story that counts.' Being Welsh I have the gene that facilitates the telling of a good story; always true, always genuine, embellished usually, hyperbole essential. I'm known for being a talker; I'm not one to be ignored if I have something to say or information to share. When I talk, people listen, I entertain. I'm by nature a vocal person and so committing pen to paper you have to imagine I'm talking directly to you. I'm no literary expert; I'm a simple storyteller. I talk in stories. This story is about my struggles with Post Traumatic Stress Disorder (PTSD), a journey into the unknown and unfamiliar places of myself. This is not a thesis on all things PTSD, it's about how I got stuck and unstuck from a cruel, disabling, emotional glue.

I share my story because I'd have put money on me never, ever suffering from mental illness. As arrogant as it sounds, for fifty years I believed I'd have won such a bet. It's not that I've had an easy life. I've had enough troubles from age seven to fifty-seven that could have easily 'sent me off the rails, 'made me lose the plot', 'go under', or 'have a nervous breakdown'. I've certainly had an eventful life. No exaggeration required, but I tally a good number of reasons from a difficult childhood, having malignant melanoma whilst pregnant, and being in a marriage that was slowly dissolving. But for most of my life I'd been able to cope. I'd been strong. I'd been resilient. I stayed positive. I stayed happy. I was still smiling, despite the shit life shovelled at me. So, believe me it's true: anyone, yes anyone, can be struck down by mental illness.

> "Behold, ye speak an idle thing:
> Ye never knew the sacred dust:
> I do but sing because I must,
> And pipe but as the linnets sing:"

From Lord Alfred Tennyson's rhymes of 1850
In Memoriam.

I'm telling this story because I want to get it out. For me, an extrovert, I have to get stuff out; talking helps me solve problems, helps me cope. Brain to mouth is cathartic. My story started as ten pages of brain dumping as I wrestled with getting understood. No matter how much I said, or how eloquently I said it, it seemed those listening to me were struggling to really get what I was saying.

Despite my verbal diarrhoea my pain was obscure. I was screaming inside but to the outside world I appeared to be coping; I was still in the driving seat. I wrote my first words to help my GP and therapist see the horrors in my head, the mess in my mind, the hate in my heart, the terror in my soul. Writing is painful. I wrote to heal myself; I wrote to help others. Words matter; I know many people truly struggle to voice their inner feelings, especially in times of pain and fear. I hope that my scribbles help those who cannot find the words they need to get recognition and support.

It's been a bloody scary journey, travelling alone in the dark, no path, no route, no destination, wandering aimlessly in pain into the unknown. Writing this gave me some definition: I've put my white pebbles down, rather like Gretel in Grimm's fairy tale, so if ever I come this way again, I can see my way back to safety. I hope my trail can be of use to others crossing the terrain of the mind with PTSD or mental illness.

Rhyme and Reason

Often times when we are sick or shit comes our way, we tend to ask ourselves, 'why me?' We ask this question in part because we do want an answer, we do want to understand, and we want to know where the problem stemmed from. Knowing why will help us prevent 'it' happening again, to us or to others. Or we ask 'why me?' as a rhetorical question: we just want to moan or signal our despair; we feel sorry for ourselves; 'woe is me' as Job and Shakespeare declared. Maybe you've picked up this book because you're asking yourself, 'Do I have PTSD?' Or maybe you are reading this because you are concerned a loved one, friend or colleague may be struggling with their mental health.

Unlike so many mental illnesses there is a valid, concrete, reason why people get PTSD. This makes understanding PTSD so much easier than, say, depression, anxiety or bipolar disorder. Before I say much more, I think it's important to emphasise that PTSD happens in response to trauma. It's not a response to the usual stresses or anxieties of daily living or our concerns over everyday pressures such as work, finances, health hiccups, relationship problems or how we look. Post Traumatic—

it's all in the name. A Top Tips document produced for GPs describes PTSD as 'a delayed and/or protracted response to a stressful event or situation of an exceptionally threatening or catastrophic nature, which is likely to cause extreme distress in almost anyone.' We all react to trauma in different ways, experiencing a range of physical and emotional reactions. There is no right or wrong way to think, feel, or respond; we are all different and the circumstances of each trauma is unique. Our initial responses are normal reactions to abnormal events. While emotional trauma is a normal response to disturbing events, it becomes PTSD when the nervous system gets stuck and we remain in psychological shock, unable to make sense of what happened or process our emotions.

There are some good resources online describing the diagnosis of PTSD and definitions of trauma, and I've listed some of these at the back of this book so I will try not to weigh things down with the techy bits from hereon in. The question I asked myself were, 'Why now? Why do I have PTSD now?' You may think this an odd question, but as Tilly (from the British sitcom TV series, Miranda) says 'bear with'. For many people who suffer PTSD, the reasons, as in the traumatic event, are obvious and for me, the first time I suffered PTSD the trauma was blatantly understandable. The second time PTSD showed up was less apparent, hence the question 'why now?'

In 2005 I began suffering PTSD after my son had a number of bad asthma attacks; attacks that put him in intensive care on life support; he had respiratory and cardiac arrests when these terrible asthma attacks struck. It was these repeated traumatic experiences that triggered PTSD as my brain struggled to process the horrific memories. The first time I witnessed my son nearly die from an asthma attack was in 2001; he was four and at the time we were told he had suffered incipient respiratory failure. Basically, his lungs were unable to do their job and he was finding it extremely hard to breath. Potentially he could have died, but he didn't, thanks to the medical team. The event was a shock but we all recovered reasonably quickly following the incident, which happened on the last day of our holiday on Guernsey. The second time he had a near fatal asthma attack he was eight; this time things were more dramatic and horrific than the earlier one. This second time he had a cardiac arrest and I watched a crash team do CPR to get him back. We were fortunate to be in hospital at the time and once the crash team had resuscitated my son the plan was to move him from the children's ward to intensive care. On the way to intensive care he had a respiratory arrest on the trolley as we sped down the long cream hospital corridor in the bowels of a major hospital. There was much more to this event than I can do justice to here, but suffice to say it was this second event in 2005 that triggered my PTSD. My son was hospitalised nearly every six weeks that year (my annus horribilis) and over the next ten years he suffered a number of life-threatening and serious asthma attacks which turned our lives upside down.

I had never felt so:
Frightened
Anxious
Numb

Over the ten years that my youngest was going in and out of hospital with these life-threatening asthma attacks I learnt to live with the flashbacks, nightmares and the compartmentalising of the pain, anxiety and fear. I was super twitchy, living in a constant red alert state, and I was easily bothered by noise and smells. I should have sought more help at the time but I didn't recognise that I had a long-term problem. Besides, I'd other more pressing things to deal with, including looking after my son, caring for my daughter (who had chronic health problems too), helping both children in the aftermath of each event, and running my own business. For a number of reasons I was the main wage earner and paying the mortgage was dependant on my income. I had to get back to work quickly after each event; no time to stop, no time to deal with my feelings, no time to heal. I thought if I kept going, the PTSD would eventually pass and time would do the mending. Big mistake. But then as we *all* know, hindsight's a wonderful thing.

Wind forward to 2019 and the PTSD is out of its box again. In the intervening years much had happened; my daughter had nearly died whilst volunteering in Ghana, and returned to the UK with seizures that were eventually diagnosed as epilepsy; my mum had a bad fall just before Christmas and following surgery died in January of 2018; my husband nearly popped his clogs in the summer of 2017 with what was quickly, thanks to me dragging him to the doctor, diagnosed as stage 4 kidney disease. Good things had come to pass too. My daughter had graduated with a First-Class Honours degree from a good London university despite crippling health issues. My son had turned out fit and well, eventually passing his driving test on the 6th attempt, got a job and gone to university. My husband and I had separated.

I know the PTSD came back with a vengeance because I'd not dealt with it first time around. I'd been cramming the pain and negative shit into my money box, burying it, ignoring it and just moving on to cope with life. I'd been doing this for so bloody long, just surviving. Just. Second time around the PTSD was far worse.

I felt:
scared,
terrified,
vulnerable,
torn,
apprehensive,
angry,
on edge,
guilty,
a failure,
exhausted,
exposed,
and sad, so sad.

The difference between my initial bout of PTSD and my more recent trouble was the intensity to which it disabled me from doing my job and living my life. First time around I managed to soldier on. The obvious PTSD symptoms of flashbacks and nightmares tended to be acute, troubling me in and around the asthma attacks, lasting for six to eight weeks at most. Second time around the symptoms were more troublesome, chronic and truly disabling; I could not cope. Second time around it took eight months before I knew I had PTSD again. During all the last twenty-five years I'd been living with an alcoholic husband. I believe I would not have suffered so long and so badly with PTSD had I had the support of my husband during the bad times and the early years of my illness. Alcohol was the barrier preventing him from being there completely and fully for us all. We came second to the addiction. Second was not enough.

When my husband and I separated in 2018 I felt relief. I knew I was doing the right thing, for me, my children and even my husband. Being separated meant I didn't have to keep pretending; pretending being to be happily married had been draining. I felt less tight. I felt less of a need to be someone I was not. I didn't need to be on guard anymore. I do think it was this release that allowed my PTSD to resurface. It was as if my body was saying 'about that roadblock, the pain of the past, the bad memories, they are still here………' Or it was simpler, my money box was full: stuffed with my pain, fear, anxiety and horrific memories there was no room for any more shit.

First Signs

For the last thirty years I'd had a successful career in the life sciences sector, having worked my way from a pharmaceutical sales representative in the Welsh valleys, to a senior executive in a global healthcare organisation. I was good at my job. I worked hard. I loved the variety, the chance to travel to amazing countries and meet inspiring people. My path had not been easy; I'd had my fair share of troubles along the way, but I always managed to stay positive. I was resilient and bounced back easily. I found ways to turn misadventures and bad luck into funny stories, with lessons to learn thrown in.

Very early in my career when I was a sales rep, I had the fortunate experience of having my appendix removed whilst on a company sales meeting to Cyprus. In the days before the trip, I'd not been 100%, having a bit of an insecure tummy. But I wasn't going to let a dodgy stomach stop me going on my first business trip abroad, no way. I took a few Imodium® tablets to settle my gut down. On the bus trip from Larnaca International Airport to the conference hotel I started to feel really sick. I assumed this was travel sickness which I was prone to on buses when not sitting by the window, and more to the point, the roads we were traveling on were horrendously winding. I felt terrible. In addition to the Imodium®, I took another remedy, Stugeron®, to settle the nausea. I knew these drugs well as they were ones I talked about to GPs and pharmacist regularly in my job as a sales rep. I was so relieved to arrive at our conference destination and took myself straight off to bed, missing the first night's fun. On our second night, as I was getting ready for the evening fancy dress function (theme based on a song), I began to feel awful. The niggling pain I'd had in my side all day began to increase in intensity and I was soon doubled up in pain. Alongside the pain came a torrent of vomiting and diarrhoea. My regional sales manager, for reasons I never understood, had chosen a Devon folk song, and had us don rough hessian smocks, straw hats and brown baggy trousers; something to do with Uncle Tom Cobley and Widecombe Fair. I looked so stupid when a local Cypriot doctor came to examine me, by now half dressed in the sack cloth with straw all over the bathroom where I'd been confined for over two hours. The doctor suspected acute appendicitis. The Medical Director (MD) of the company I was working for at the time suspected inflamed gall bladder. I was in so much pain I didn't care what was removed, I'd have said yes to anything. I needed surgery quickly and it was decided not to attempt getting to the main hospital. The local doctor suggested I be taken to his vasectomy clinic, just up the road, to get further tests to confirm which bit to dig out and then he would operate. I was a little bit anxious by now as we were in a remote part of Cyprus and I was worried this doctor might not have a proper set up or staff for surgery of any kind, appendix or gall bladder. I worried I may even have to be awake to have an operation if they did not have an anaesthetist.

Although bloody scary I was lucky enough to be seen and operated on by this smart doctor whom I later learnt was a surgeon specialising in vasectomy and cleft palate. He was truly skilled at the most delicate of operations, a plastic surgeon who'd trained in London and I was safe in his hands. I certainly didn't want the MD to operate on me. He had offered. But seeing as it had been a while since he had been a practising surgeon I declined; besides which he had offered to remove my gall bladder, having misdiagnosed the problem. Imagine a young woman (me) in a six-bed vasectomy clinic in an isolated region of Cyprus. Despite my not speaking Greek, I was spoilt rotten by the wives of the male patients (through pigeon English and much gesticulation) who brought me food, flowers and much needed female products (don't ask, use your imagination). Having had abdominal surgery, I was compelled to stay in Cyprus for over a week before flying home. It so happened that two of my colleagues also had been hospitalised during the sales meeting: one for asthma and the other for a serious head injury after a stupid diving stunt. All three of us were left under the charge a healthy, sensible, senior colleague, in a remote villa in a beautiful part of the island while we all recuperated and all paid for by the company travel insurance. Bum deal, eh? I was glad my appendix played up when it had; I now had the neatest and smallest scar of any appendectomy. On getting checked up when I got back to the UK my GP commented that had this happened while home, in all likelihood my appendix would have been removed by a junior doctor who needed the surgical practice, and the scar would have been three times as long and much more pronounced. Every cloud has a silver lining. Nothing to complain about: I even got my silk underwear replaced courtesy of the insurance claim (because my own had only been rolled down and not removed during the surgery, and the iodine used had ruined them).

Two years later I went for a job interview at another pharmaceutical company, and was answering a question about the most challenging thing I'd dealt with at work. I told the Cyprus appendix story as this was now a well-tuned tale. I ended by saying something about reading the signs, learning my lesson in self-medicating, not being over confident and trusting others to make the right decisions. As I was speaking, I could see the interviewer look at me in amazement. I was puzzled. This was an unusual tale and when I tell it with all the gesticulation it's funny. But it's not that incredible. I worried she did not believe me. Then she burst out laughing. I was so nervous. I thought I'd lost my chance at this great new job to be a clinical research scientist. At last the interviewer came clean and explained she'd heard this story a few times before, as my previous MD had told it during after-dinner speaking engagements. He'd beefed up his role in the saga, but in essence the story was the same. At the time she'd first heard the tale she'd thought it was a gross exaggeration, with very little truth to it. Guess what? I got the job and the chance to share more of the gruesome and comic details over a bottle of wine.

Back to now, it's the early part of the year (2019) and I'm working in a consultancy business, busily planning and preparing for the coming years' future success, driven by getting business in, making the right hires and managing our resources effectively. I usually find this time to be an exciting part of the year; building on the experience of the previous year (good and bad), developing new strategies to grow the business, justifying budget requests and implementing staff hiring plans. I normally thrive at the beginning of the year, there is so much to do. As a senior executive, my role is a visible one, with responsibility and accountability; I love setting the stage, sharing the vison, negotiating terms, supporting staff, delivering the goods and solving problems. I get a buzz from the environment in which I work, it's global, so I get to travel regularly to the US, India and Europe. The work is technical and so I get to work with bright minds and creative people; our sector deals with health and thus I know we are making a difference to people's lives; our sector is evolving, I'm never bored, there are plenty of new challenges to address even after decades in the business. I'm so often the catalyst for shared success and working as part of a team is stimulating on so many levels. I'm blessed with a natural energy, healthy competitive nature and so comfortable in dealing with people. I'm fortunate to have a career I enjoy and am competent at.

But this year things are different. I wake up scared. I feel anxious as soon as I open my eyes. I'm nervous for no reason. I feel like disaster is about to strike. I feel as if there is doom pending around the corner. I feel sad deep in my bones. I want to hide. I'm awash with negative emotions. I'm overwhelmed by the strength of these feelings. I've never known anything like this before. I'm a born optimist, I'm irritatingly positive, I always find a way to smile and see the sun. I'm not enjoying things. I'm not comfortable, not one bit. As February goes by, I know I'm struggling but I decide the best thing to do is to keep going. I tell myself this is a phase, a natural response to the fact that in the prior six months my husband and I had separated. Every morning I make myself get up, get out of bed; I wash and shower, make sure I look good: make up on, hair done, flattering clothes, keep smiling. My mantra:

Keep smiling.
Keep going.
Block the negative shit out.
Don't feel it.
Don't give in.
Keep busy.
Keep it out.
Keep smiling.

As February goes on it's getting harder and harder to block the negative shit out. At work I start to panic about talking to colleagues and chairing meetings. I cannot make decisions quickly; I worry about any decisions I have to make. I'm confused; for over thirty years I've been in the front line of the business and never been muddled or nervous. I do most routine things automatically and am quick to act. I'm normally objective and decisive. Now I can't think clearly. I'm apprehensive of people. The apprehension is a worry in itself. This is not me. This is so not me.

> I doubt my competence.
> I cannot think clearly.
> I find myself hiding in the toilets.
> I'm petrified of talking to clients.
> When the phone rings I physically jump.
> I push on, keep going.
> I recite my mantra.

That February I did a two-week business development trip to the USA with a colleague. At Heathrow, despite having a wonderful time in the snazzy airline members' lounge, I feel the panic begin rise. I don't want to get on the plane; I cannot do two weeks on the road, talking to clients, selling, consulting, solving problems, discussing new ideas, securing business and doing my job. I can't. I try to think of any excuse not to get on the plane.

I can't do it.
I'm so scared.
Not sure exactly what I'm scared of.
I'm drowning in fear.
I got on the plane.
I did all that was required of me.
I did my job.

To the outside world, colleagues and clients I was the usual me. During those two weeks I hid so often in the toilet, thinking of any reason not to walk into the next meeting. I felt vulnerable; I thought people could see through me and know I was weak; see I was scared. I recited my mantra over and over to get through each day. On the flight home I decide to confide in my colleague; I explained what I'd been feeling and how this impacted on my behaviour; to my surprise my colleague had no idea I'd been through this turmoil. At least my mantra was helping, or so I thought at the time. Over the next six months I lived by my mantra. I got up and performed my duties. I worked hard at being me. I worked hard to keep smiling. I started walking more on my days off. I hoped to march away the fear and anxiety, to drive the impending doom away with every footstep. At work I drove myself harder. After a driving hard spell, I'd feel exhausted and could not contain the negative emotions no matter how hard I tried. I needed to escape before I burst and so would take time off at short notice. I was not aware at the time I was swinging between over-trying and hiding away. I'd have spells of pushing myself extra hard at work, starting earlier, finishing later, and taking on more; forcing things through aggressively; not leaving anything on the backburner, getting so much done. I was like a dynamo for brief periods and then the doubt and fear would snuff all the drive out and I'd be immobilised by the fear. Once I hit a bad spell, I'd take a day or two off work, so I could hide away. This pattern went on throughout the spring and summer. Hiding how I truly felt was exhausting; physically and mentally. I ached with the burden of hiding the pain and fear. I was physically and mentally drained. I was so tired. I felt like an old dishcloth, all wrung out. I feel I'm going mad. I'm so tired of trying to keep sane; my head hurts with the thoughts, images and feelings bouncing around my skull. I get muddled so easily. I can't think straight some days. I can't make simple decisions. My head spins and spins with thoughts, sometimes I think I'm okay, I am getting better, then the next minute I'm pushing down the bad stuff. I work so hard at blocking the bad stuff out, on thinking good thoughts only. Thinking, too much thinking, pushing thoughts away. The bouts of numbness, feeling flat and sad make me feel weirdly safe with the lack of the high intensity emotion. Weird, makes me think I'm mad, cracking up big time. Bring on the white coats.

What do I do? I make myself think rationally, but the negative feelings are crippling, they're disabling me.

I can't think.
I can't think.
I can't think.

I try to convince myself that my thoughts are **not** facts. Most days I can't make the simplest of decisions, never mind anything important or complex. When my son was growing up, I read, and reread, watched, and re-watched, R. R. Tolkien's epic stories. I felt like Bilbo-Baggins when he tells Gandalf, in A Long-expected Party, The Fellowship of the Ring, 'Why, I feel all thin, sort of stretched, if you know what I mean: like butter that has been scraped over too much bread. That can't be right. I need a change, or something.' In recognition I probably could benefit from a change or something, I decided to book myself on an organised group trip with a well-known travel company whom I'd travelled to Vietnam with in the previous November. In less than an hour after looking on line at some great destinations I landed on a ten-day trip to Jordan for September. I decided this was good timing to get used to my new circumstances; my son was moving to a new job and thus leaving home. It all made perfect sense to me. A break, a holiday, an adventure; something to look forward to, time away from work and my troubles, the answer to my feeling thin. This was going to be a busy month with the moving out and me travelling for a few weeks, I'd need some extended leave; restorative time for me, time to recharge. Surely this would be the answer: a good rest, a change.

For this extended break from work I'd need agreement from colleagues and thus I discussed my plans with HR. Smiling, putting on my brave face I explained how my responsibilities would be covered while I was away in the sure knowledge my extended break would be sanctioned. I deserved it; I'd worked hard and achieved much in the year to date. 'So, what I'm asking for is just over four weeks off, from the August Bank Holiday to the end of September. I've organised cover for all my projects and clients and my team know what to do while I'm away. Five weeks off, OK, Agreed?' I was dumfounded when my colleague replied with a firm, flat 'no'. I felt myself crumbling, I felt tears building up. Where had my plan gone wrong? What was the problem I'd not foreseen?

How can she say no? And more to the point, no to me. My colleague had spotted my behaviour of late and was concerned I was struggling. It was not that my leave was to be denied, it was more that she wanted me to take some time out, some sick leave and seek help. I thought I'd done a great job of keeping my pain, and distress hidden. However, I was now exposed. I couldn't hide anymore. I realised then I didn't really want to hide anymore.

I wanted to stop.
I wanted the pain to stop.
I wanted support.
I wanted help.
I wanted to deal with the fear.

I admitted I was struggling and agreed to see my GP. We had a plan and I felt positive. Time off work, with my trip to Jordan part of the therapy; in no time I'd be back to being super Me, always smiling, always coping, never frightened. If only.

This insightful caring person had my well-being at heart and she was instrumental in kick starting my journey out of PTSD. I realise with hindsight how courageous this woman was; when I thanked her, she told me she was just doing her job. But she was doing more than her job, more than just being a professional: she was being human; she was being a friend. She took a risk tackling me on this, my response could have been either to bite her head off or make a joke of it (deflecting emotional anguish with humour as the psychologist call it). This beautiful brave human being remains a friend to this day.

September came, my son moved out; I felt proud he was making his own way in the world. I was also selfishly pleased as this gave me a good excuse to get my sewing machine out to make curtains for his new home. I love sewing and as a pretty good seamstress, having designed and made my own wedding dress, I get great satisfaction out of running up decent, well lined pairs of curtains. I get high on the smell of the fabric and love the reassurance heavy drapes offer on cold winter nights. But before the sewing could begin, I had my trip to the Middle East to enjoy. And I did enjoy my trip to Jordan. Petra blew my mind, along with the aridness of the country. The trip was ideal. I'd nothing to fear, all I had to do was turn up at the airport. From there on everything was organised. All I had to do was choose what to wear and what to eat. No decisions harder than that. The company of my fellow travellers was great. I had nothing to trigger my fear and anxiety, or so I thought. All was fine until two days before the end of the trip. Whilst dining out one warm evening when camping in the Wadi Rum desert, one of my fellow travellers shared the news with me that the group had decided I was the best person to organise the collection for our guide and driver. This simple task meant collecting the donations from the group and giving a little thank you speech on the last night. I felt sick. I felt all the panic and fear come back. This was madness. Surely, I could collect the donations and give a suitable thank you? I am Me. I'm organised. I'm eloquent. I don't dodge responsibility. I wanted to say no. I had a choice after all. I wanted to be honest to myself and just say no; no, I can't, no I don't want to. No, no, no. But I remembered my mantra and so did what was required and expected of me. My default setting:

Keep going.
Keep smiling.
Keep coping.

At the airport for the flight home, I confided in the person who'd asked me to do the honours of the collection. I explained how I'd felt and the person was shocked to know I'd felt anything other than relaxed and natural. Relaxed. Natural?

Me on show.
Me performing.
Me hiding her true self.
Hiding.
Hiding.

Is that natural?

More Signs

There were other signs I was not myself in 2019.

I could not:
Make decisions
Concentrate
Sit at the PC for very long

I'm one of those people who tend to be on or off, in or out. I rarely sit on the fence. I rarely hold back on expressing my opinion. I'm someone who is very comfortable making decisions. Too comfortable it seems. In my late twenties when working as a junior clinical research scientist, my boss suggested at one of our annual performance reviews that I go on a decision-making course. I looked aghast at him. I was confused. 'I'm the most prolific and effective decision maker in the team. I never dilly dally making a decision' I wailed. 'Yes,' my boss agreed, 'that's your problem. You make your decisions too quickly and you make decision that are for others to make'. My natural style needed to be honed; I gladly attended the course. I came to understand what decisions were mine to take and which were not; I learnt how to influence those with authority and power. I found this course a real help, quite liberating, as it meant I had licence to back off or back out. I do have to catch myself still; I'm still by nature a natural decision maker.

Back to 2019, and I'm choked with anxiety about making the simplest of decisions. Leave alone the complex decisions I have to make every day at work; I cannot even decide if I should put petrol in the car at the BP or the Shell garage. I can't decide which plumber from the Checkatrader leaflet to call to fix my broken boiler. I can't decide if I should have the septic tank emptied on a Monday or Thursday. I can't work out the best way to manage my finances on the internet banking. Food shopping is painfully slow, despite going in with a list, as I aimlessly wander around the aisles trying to choose tins of tomatoes, breakfast cereals or bloody toilet rolls. I can't decide where to park the car when I'm out shopping: the Pay and Display, the underground supermarket carpark or the two-hour free area by Matalan, resulting in me driving around roundabouts multiple times, until someone beeps me into a decision.

Work is a nightmare; people look to me to take the lead, to come up with ideas, to have opinions, but I'm silent. I've nothing to say. I can't process problems no matter how hard I try. I stall. I hesitate. I defer. I avoid being the one to make the call. I delegate more. I don't highlight issues as much as I did. I leave things be. Dealing with clients becomes something I truly dread. Clients expect me to make decisions. I try taking a more consultative approach to hide my inability—'what were you thinking we should try first? Would you like more time to think?' or I defer the conversation altogether, pushing meetings into the far future and making them shorter so there is less chance to talk. I found concentrating hard, both at work and at home. I'd lose track and things did not seem to go in. I had to repeat things many times to get something done. I'd read chapters of books three times. I'd take an hour to write an email that usually took 10 minutes. I couldn't get a grip with new systems, Apps or tech. I struggled with sorting the Wi-Fi out at home. I forgot passwords. Words seemed to go in one ear and out the other. If people at work thought I was going deaf, I don't blame them as I said 'pardon' more than ever. I made a silly mistake knitting a cardigan; I wrongly calculated the amount of wool I needed. I'd knitted this cardigan twice before; it's made as one piece. I needed five 100 gm balls. I knitted away for hours. But I'd only bought five 50 gm balls. I ended up with half a cardigan. I was not able to source an additional five balls to finish the job. A perfectly symmetrical half garment in pure wool. Plenty of famous artists leave works unfinished: look at Leonardo da

Vinci, Titian and Schubert for example; experts love them for it, the mystery, and the unanswered questions. I ended up casting off and keeping the unfinished garment for posterity, a reminder of my difficult days with PTSD. It makes me laugh every time I look at it.

I made date, tomato and apple chutney that autumn and by mistake put 10 ozs of salt in with the painstakingly chopped fruit and onions instead of 1 oz. I've followed the recipe over fifty times, and even when I poured out the mountain of salt, I didn't register my mistake. It was only when I licked my finger while filling the jars, I realised what a waste: waste of time; waste of good food; waste of effort. I burst into tears; I felt so stupid, so wasteful. I never would have cried over something so silly before. I ended up throwing my concoction on the garden in frustration and self-pity: it turned out to be great deterrent for slugs and super composting. When travelling to friends for lunch just before the Covid lockdown in March of 2020 I was ninety minutes late. I had stupidly driven three junctions past where I should have come off, making my journey over sixty miles longer. I've done that journey hundreds of times over the last thirty years and never made such an error. It was as if I was on autopilot with my brain switched off. I was so focused on driving safely on the motorway that my capacity to navigate was swamped under the concentration. Thankfully, my friends understood, lunch was not ruined and we laughed that at least I had not gone any further.

I have never been a big fan of shops. In truth I particularly resent the time spent on food shopping, only to have to repeat the exercise again and again, week after week. Even internet grocery shopping is as tedious, Luckily, my husband had been more than happy to take over the food shopping duties for the majority of our married life. But now we were separated, if I was going to eat I needed to take responsibility for sourcing the goods. By now I could not handle any shops at all. I'd get panic attacks as soon as I entered any type of store. In supermarkets I found myself pushing the trolley aimlessly through the aisles. I could not read my shopping list and manoeuvre to the right shelf or section of the store. I could not choose the items, too many brands, too many choices, advertising attacking my decisions. I found the other customers came too near, pressing into my personal space, invading my zone. I wanted to scream 'go away'. I would eat everything in the cupboards and freezer, down to the last morsel to avoid going shopping. It's sad and ironic that the phrase 'retail therapy' was first used in the 1986 to decry 'comfort buying'. Shopping is not therapy of any kind. It is torture for many of us with mental illness. To spend is not to mend.

Scared and Screaming

The fear is overwhelming; it stops me from thinking, making decisions and thus taking action. Fear gets in the way of being in control; being scared all the time makes it difficult for me to get perspective. Fear prevents me from prioritising, balancing and judging. Being scared slows everything down; everything takes longer as I swim through the fog of fear. It's all so exhausting. I feel like I'm running on cheap batteries, I'm going to be flat soon.

I feel afraid.
I feel terrified.
I'm scared. Truly scared.
Scared my son will die.
Scared my daughter will die.
Scared my son's next asthma attack will kill him.
Scared my daughter's next epilepsy attack will kill her.
Scared I won't be able to save them.
Afraid of everything.
Afraid, scared, terrified.

I walk around with the fear every day; I wear it like a cloak. It feels like a part of me and yet not a part of me.

It feels real, heavy. It's as if this dark mantle is only inches away from my body, I can feel its weight, its oppressive weight, bearing down on my body. On bad days it's an unbearable burden; on better days if feels like a dark shadow. It's always present. I recall doing a short video in 2006 for Asthma UK (I was a research and policy volunteer for the charity for a number of years) describing these feelings of dread; many people who watched it contacted me commenting on how tangible my fear was. When I spoke at Asthma UK meetings about this fear, fear of death in the main at this time, audiences would cry. In the end I stopped doing these communications as I couldn't handle other people's emotional response; it emphasised the reality of the terror my family and I were living with. Although our story helped people realise that asthma can kill and this in itself led to a number of positive changes in asthma care and policy, retelling of our experiences was draining me. My habit of a lifetime has been to put 'bad' stuff away. I'd park the negative feelings away into compartments, it was easier that way:

Bury them

Best forget that all together / There is no time or room for feeling that way at all / Those sorts of feeling do no one any good

Token touch

Got that it's sad, but don't dwell on it / There is no time or room for feeling that way for too long / best look forward / let's deal with it later

Analyse them

Take the emotion out of this / let's look at this logically, objectively / there is no reason to feel this way

This fear and dread are too strong to compartmentalise and I can't keep the lid on them. I can't seem to cram the negativity into the compartments; it keeps bursting out.

Negative emotions bursting out:

Fear
Petrified my children will die
Anger
Hate
Sadness
Hyper-twitchy
Self-doubt
Pain
Regret
Wanting to hide
Anxiety
Aggression
Flat
Emptiness
Pathetic
Lack of concentration
Irrational thoughts
Restless and twitchy
Nervous

I feel I'm a burden. I don't want to be a burden for my children. I want to be strong for them not scared. I want to see a wonderful future for us all but I'm very frightened. I have irrational thoughts that things will go wrong for my children. I worry they will be sick and die, my daughter with her epilepsy and my son with his asthma. I have horrid nightmares my kids die in a car accident.

Anger

Anger and hate, the emotions I work hardest to keep out. They are new and uncomfortable feelings; my anger is intensely visceral; my hate is abhorrent. I can't move forward with a divorce from my husband if I'm angry and allow the hate to direct the conversation and future. But god am I ANGRY. I have to keep it out of my thinking, I really have to. I respond too hard—too much anger and frustration in my head. I'm angry that life's not going to plan. I'm such a planner and I tried hard to stay married. Misplaced emotion, misplaced anger. I'm an emotional person; I do have passion; I'm someone who generates excitement; I'm often the catalyst for things, at work and at home. I have energy, buckets full. At my lowest moments I could not control these distressing emotions. I was confused because in parallel I felt flat, sad, and lonely inside (even though I have many friends and great colleagues). I felt overwhelming hate and anger, sometimes specifically towards my husband for the things that drove me to ask him to leave. I found the hate and anger awful to admit even to myself, the depths of them so deep and physical in a horrid way. I felt ashamed of these feelings; they were repulsive and destructive. So un-me.

There was not always a target or rationale for my anger. Some days I'd wake up and the anger would build slowly, starting with feeling irritable; ratty for no reason. My fuse seemed shorter. I could feel an aggression taking over and it was during these moments I was prone to swearing unnecessarily. At work my emails became clipped, and rather than point out my colleague's errors with tact and diplomacy, I'd hit them hard with cruel words, a figurative slap in the face. It was all the harsher as I didn't bother to remove those cc'd onto the mail trail. Luckily for most of this period my youngest, who was living with me at the time, was working shifts and our paths crossed little and this saved me from lashing out at him. I recall being quite rude to a bank teller who was chewing gum and talking to her colleague whilst serving me; grounds to be disappointed with customer service but not to the extent I voiced my displeasure. I even complained to her manager: I was so angry and the poor girl was in my sights from the moment I stepped into the bank and saw her grazing like a cow.

Irritability and anger were feelings that often came together, like terrible twins aggravating each other. I hated the person I became when this happened, I felt cold and hard. This was not Me. I became intolerant of silly things; things that never bothered me before. I hated mess, crumbs on a table, dishes left on the kitchen unit, toothpaste splashes on the bathroom mirror, food stains on my kitchen floor, untidy desks at work, litter bugs, badly parked cars, people eating with their mouth open, pedestrians not walking straight on the pavement and dog owners not cleaning up their dogs' poo. I was coming out of London one evening after work and being rush hour the Oxford Tube bus service was busy. I got on the coach at Marble Arch and headed upstairs in the hope of a window seat. I was lucky to find a free seat by the window half way along the coach, but by the time we left Shepherds Bush the coach was full. In the eighty minutes it took to get to my stop I was frothing with irritability. The irritation was so strong I had to sit on my hands to stop myself slapping the woman who had plonked herself next to me. I could not escape the awful smells from her snacks; she was a noisy eater, crunching her crisps, munching her wrap, slurping her coke, sucking her Frubes® yogurt. I wanted to scream. My blood was boiling and my nerves were tight. My fists and jaw were locked with inner tension. I could not breathe my way out of this torture. Eventually, I spent the journey with my fingers in my ears, wishing I had a pair of headphones (like my kids had been nagging me to get, since I'd been trapped listening to a garrulous and boring person on another bus journey out of London the week before.). That lady had no idea how lucky she was not to be assaulted physically or verbally by me that evening. It was a horrible experience. Eighty minutes of intense irritability was hell, and left me exhausted. I'm not one to resort to alcohol when there is trouble at t'mill, but that night as soon as I got home, I had a large glass of wine and went straight to bed.

Building up with anger, simmering with anger, brimming with anger, blowing up in anger, reaching boiling point, erupting with anger, getting hot under the collar. Perfect verbs. Taking the heat out of my anger was impossible; I was like a latent volcano most of the time; quiet on the outside, my destructive energy bubbling beneath the surface. Can you tell a volcano to calm down? My outbursts of anger even caught me by surprise in terms of their ferocity. It's draining being angry so much; it saps your emotional reserves. Anger makes you feel ashamed after a while. I could not claim righteous anger; my anger and irritability were destructive and so not me. My anger and irritability were like bad breath; I was acutely aware of it; I was also aware others were aware of it too; it sometimes caused people to keep their distance, all too polite to say anything or offer help. Literally, foul mouth.

Sadness

There were days I felt sad, so sad and on those days in 2019-2020 I allowed myself to stay at home (always dressed, not a pyjama or track suit in sight) and cry. Cry, cry, cry. It was cathartic. I was not ashamed to cry for hours. But I'd only cry alone. I found it hard, nigh on impossible to cry in front of others; I worked hard not to cry in public. I'd cry for no reason, I'd just cry. Although I'd good reason to be sad at this time, the sadness like the anger, felt irrational, disconnected to any specific event. I learnt to accept this and not feel guilty 'about wasting time moping'. I just felt sad. Truly and absolutely sad. Sad for no reason. That's OK, today we have sadness on the agenda. Most days I could not think about the past that's not why I cried. When I did think about the past, I recognised it was understandable to feel sadness and regret; but the depths of my remorse were cavernous, something I'd never felt before. I wished I'd made different decisions. I was sad my marriage had failed. Sad that all the time, effort and love had not helped keep us afloat as a couple, a happy family. Sad drink and addiction appeared to have won, consumed a person, destroyed a marriage, and caused pain for my children and me.

The sadness physically hurt. My body ached, my limbs felt tender and heavy. The sadness held me down like a ball and chain; I was its prisoner.

I felt:
damaged
bruised
loss
grief
confused
despair

On my sad days I'd listen to melancholy music, not to make it worse or wallow in my misery, but to give voice to my blues; allow myself the time to really feel, and to create an avenue for getting my feelings out. Out. Out. Freeing them. Freeing me.

I cannot sing. At school I was sent out of music lessons by my teacher, Mr Fewster, at least once a month: the guy could not believe I was tone deaf and thought I was messing about. I was a grade A student in every other subject, so why would I play up in music? When asked to sing scales I just screeched louder. Pitch, scale, tone, major, minor I didn't understand any of it; I couldn't hear what everyone else seemed to. I sound like a dying dog when singing. But an enthusiastic dying dog to be fair. Despite my lack of ability, I was put in the school choir for the Welsh National Eisteddfod competitions. Being short I was put in the front row and told to mime the reason being, I had an expressive face and my teachers believed my animated expressions could swing the judges. It was true: I endured being poked in the back by the girls in the second row if I as much uttered a word aloud. Miming is no fun. But we won often enough for me to endure the secret humiliation. Despite his skill I know Gareth Malone would fail to remedy my un-Welshness.

Although I've no musical talent, I nevertheless love singing and dancing, I just have to do it alone, to spare others the pain. I often pour my heart out with a good tune in the car or in my lounge. Singing and dancing are therapeutic, and I found sad songs drew out my gloomy emotions and stopped them clogging up my veins. If I wanted a good sob, a melancholy moment, a cathartic cry, I'd howl, sway and hum to emotionally infused music. The music I bathed myself in at these sad times touched a space deep inside me. The music spoke to me. It said 'I get your pain. I know it hurts. I know what it feels like. Listen. Feel. I will surround you with empathy. I give sound to your sadness. I have been there too. I am with you now. You are not alone.'

My sad song companions:

Madame Butterfly opera, especially Un bel dì vedremo	Giacomo Puccini
Agnus Dei + Adagio for strings	Samuel Barber
Benedictus	Karl Jenkins
Skinny Love	Bonn Ivor
Schindler's List	John Williams
The Mission	Ennio Morricone
Nothing Compares to you	Sinéad O'Connor
Ave Maria	Schubert (sung by Pavarotti)
Spiegel im Spiegel	Arvo Pärt
November	Max Richter (played by Mari Samuelsen)
Fix You	Coldplay
Let her go	Passenger
Tears in Heaven	Eric Clapton
How to save a life	The Fray
Lovin' You	Minnie Riperton
Everybody hurts	R.E.M.

*'One fine day we'll see a trail of smoke
rising from the edge of the sea'*
Translation from *Madam Butterfly*

Hyper

I was in a constant state of alert—always in amber—revving, ready to go. I felt like a sprinter on the starting blocks, nervous, tense, alert and ready to spring at the first sound of the starting gun. I used to think this was normal and healthy—it was about being prepared. Prepared for trouble, because my life of the last fifteen years had been a series of troublesome events—one thing after another—this was my norm, my default setting. Best to be ready; best to be one step ahead. Expect shit, be realistic, I know trouble is coming, it always does and you have to deal with it, there is no one else. A fifteen-year-old habit, well honed. Added to the readiness was a sense of dread; dread of something awful around the corner. These feeling reminded me of the time we took a trip to London's Chamber of Horrors at Madam Tussauds when the children were young; much to the embarrassment of my kids I'd screamed before the horrors even appeared, having shrieked when the guide asked for our tickets. I was on edge as we walked through the tunnels, crying out needlessly or for the slightest hint of darkness, so much so that I was scaring the other visitors more than the ghouls and ghosts on display. Many months into my journey with PTSD I read Matt Haig's book, Notes on a Nervous Planet; he talks about anxiety as 'Invisible sharks', and he's got it spot on when he says 'It's all intense suspense, no action. It's like Jaws without the shark.' ((c) Matt Haig, 2018 Extracts from Notes on a Nervous Planet reproduced with permission of Canongate Books Ltd.) Psycho without Norman Bates, Dr Who without the Daleks, Lord of the rings without the Nazgûl, Jurassic Park without T-Rex and Harry Potter without the Dementors.

I felt like a wound-up Jack-in-the-box, a fully
loaded bow and arrow, an elastic band pulled taught
I felt overly:
Tense
Alert
On edge
On guard
Tight
Primed
Urgent
Ready
So bloody ready.........
For what?

I realised this hyper-alert state was becoming a problem when my son's budgie died. Shortly after his much-loved pet passed away, I moved straight into next steps mode, straight to action, suggesting how he handle his grief, and make plans for getting a new budgie. My son firmly asked me to stop, stop talking, stop organising; he pointed out this problem was not mine to deal with. He wanted time to grieve, he wasn't ready or in the mood to think about what to do next. More importantly he pointed out I really didn't need to spend my time or energy on this with everything else I had on my plate. It was for him to deal with the situation. 'End of' as the kids say; he quite rightly helped me realise I tend to go immediately into solution mode. All I needed to do was listen, allow him to be sad and deal with it in his own way and time. So, I did just that, I backed out and he dealt with things. A few weeks later he happily brought home a new white female budgie, Gwen (meaning white in Welsh). She still lives with me.

I struggle with the hyper-alertness; I expect trouble, I anticipate bad stuff. I'm shovel-ready. There is a pattern to my shit shovelling. I've a well-worn process which goes like this:

- Define the extent of the problem
- Define options for resolution—poor, reasonable, good, better, best

- Decide which option has legs
- Create action plan for option
- Implement action plan without delay
- Problem solved

At no point in my response is there time to feel; in fact, there is a hidden first step:

- Park your feelings, don't let emotion get in the way; put the bad stuff in the money box, lock it away—be logical. Move on.

I thought this way of dealing with life events was good, effective, productive, rational and sensible. Little did I realise I was storing up problems for my future by not recognising and dealing with my feelings. In work I'd been nicknamed firewoman as I was often the one to deal with many of our heated moments; I joked about wanting a uniform, a badge, a red engine and a company hose. But at home I was still on high alert, ready to jump into my fire engine anytime, ready to get the hose out and dampen down the non-existent blaze. I was feeling jumpy and easily startled. When Christmas food shopping in a middle-class supermarket I was standing quietly next to our trolley as a gentleman reached over to the shelf besides me. With no thought or delay, I swung my trolley around, aimed it directly at him and shoved him into the shelving on the other side of the aisle. It was only once I'd pinned him to the toothpaste shelf and saw the look of surprise on his and my daughters' face, I realised I'd overreacted. Somewhere in my head I thought the man was reaching for my handbag which was hooked on my trolley. In reality, he was reaching for the Christmas crackers. Fortunately, we managed to laugh and as no harm was done my apologies were accepted with good grace. Happy Christmas from someone with PTSD.

In work, seated at my desk when people came up behind me quietly, I was susceptible to screeching. When a colleague (who only needed to ask me a quick question) came up behind me in our workplace kitchen, I dropped a full bowl of soup (thankfully cold), splashing his new suede top of the range trainers. In the end my colleagues stomped and whistled so I had fair warning they were coming. We have electric gates at our home and it's not often our front doorbell gets used. But on the odd occasion when the gate is open people can come directly to the front door and ring our bell. The surprise in combination with my hyper-twitch state led to many comic scenarios of me screaming hysterically at the person at the door. In hindsight it was funny but at the time it was disconcerting for all delivery people, postmen, the window cleaner, electric meter reading man (I've never seen a woman read my meter in 30 years of home ownership) and any visitors. Out walking in the Chilterns, cyclists who'd come up behind me silently witnessed my screaming at close range; what are they to expect when they don't use a bell. My screams are truly blood curdling, many a Lycra® clad bloke has fallen off his bike in utter surprise; some were genuinely sorry to have startled me, and some just thought I was crazy. A fifteen-year-old habit is hard to break.

OTT Anxiety

My definition of anxiety had always been 'worry with no reason' or 'winding yourself up'. If I ever had reason to consider anxious thoughts, I tended to reframe them not because I was ashamed to be anxious but to me anxiety had no role to play in helping me get things done or survive something 'not so nice'. My vocabulary tended to be:

Concern
Worried
Nervous
Apprehensive
Doubtful
Uneasy
Cautious
Unsure

Such words suggested to me I'd a valid reason to feel that way. They were part of the normal scale of human negative emotions, all healthy, all natural and helpful; allowing me to take appropriate action. Times I might feel this way might include exams, driving tests, job interviews, giving birth, having a mammogram or surgery to remove bits, going to the dentist or on any ride at Thorpe Park and teaching your kids to drive. All quite reasonable times to feel those butterflies in your stomach, the lump in your throat, the sweaty palms or wanting to wee every five minutes.

Yet now (2019) I can't think, and yet I over think. My head is busy all the time. I can't focus. I can't get my mind to stay on topic. I panic. I've got, or will get, things wrong. My thoughts are like scrambled egg. It's easy to do physical things: making bread, cooking, making curtains for my son's new home, cleaning the house and gardening. But even reading a book, or sorting out paperwork is difficult—I fail to concentrate. I hate turning the PC on. Even when I do manage to get to it, I find I've not registered the facts and have to reread things. I try to take it slow. I spend more time on checking things and not doing things in parallel. I don't multi task anymore; it sort of helps lessen the panic if I take on one thing at a time and also ask others to check things for, or with me, when I can. I struggle to read; I listen to audio books instead and find this helpful, taking my mind off my lack of concentration. Anxiety is a great diluter of attention: anxiety thins and stretches out my thoughts and drags my decisions out of reach. I try hard to reach for my thoughts, pull them back and keep them together in a tight bundle in my hands; in my control. The anxiety pushes them out as it sits and dumps itself in the middle of my head; it's as invasive as a sumo wrestler plonking himself in a baby bath.

I recalled a friend whose son had had meningitis as a baby, and several years on she was still extremely anxious about it, despite her son being a robust, healthy and perfectly happy chap. To my mind this had been a one-off event; the outcome had been good, and the chances of her son getting meningitis again were negligible. I was saddened and somewhat frustrated that this mum was trapped by this anxiety and wasting her time (to my way of thinking) on an emotion that didn't deserve it. I recall this frustration acutely because at the time my son had just been hospitalised in ITU for the second time with a life-threatening asthma attack. The first attack had happened when he was four and I honestly believed it was just a one-off event, bad luck and bad timing or a series of unfortunate events (as we coined it at the time in honour of the Lemony Snicket books we were reading with the children). Between the first and second attack I was not anxious about it happening again, in part because I'm a born optimist, and in part because we had put in place steps to manage the asthma and anxiety had no role to play. I'd used my time and energy to make sure we all moved on from that first event. The second event was a little more challenging to bounce back from but we did it for a while. We managed not to be anxious until asthma attack number 3. By this point I realised it was not only anxiety I was feeling; after all I'd good reason to be anxious, I was feeling scared. I was feeling afraid. I was afraid my child would die next time he had an asthma attack. I felt the fear like a black heavy cloak on my shoulders. I could taste the fear in my mouth like dark blood. My heart felt like leaden concrete, heavy in my chest. Fear and anxiety are a lethal cocktail, making your palms sweat, heart race, stomach turn, and turning your legs to jelly. It's exhausting and it blinded me. I struggled to see reality; I had no room for empathy, hence my unkind thoughts about my friend's angst. Today, I am ashamed of my lack of understanding. How dare I judge someone whose trapped pain was obvious to me; it could well have been that my friend was truly struggling with the fear that her son, too, might die. Anxiety is not rational; I know that now.

I've heard myself say so often 'I don't do anxiety'; it has never been part of my makeup. I've never had to deal with it. It was not an emotion I felt much until my kids were sick. The anxiety got me big time as part of my PTSD first time around. To me anxiety meant feeling scared or nervous when you had no valid reason to be, when logically there was nothing to be afraid of and on balance the thing you were most worried about, taken to its extreme, was not likely to happen—odds on, all was going to be fine. Example, I was quite happy to send my daughter walking to school on her own, age eight, despite every other mother anxious that the Soham killer was about the strike in our town. Logic told me it was safe; my daughter was not in danger. I need not be anxious and I wasn't. I really wasn't.

Neither was I worried when, unplanned, I ended up giving birth at home with no one to help but my husband. It was child number two. I'd done childbirth before. I'd only woken my husband up two hours before giving birth as I'd not wanted to disturb my 2-year-old daughter. My husband was from farming stock and had seen births before (including child number one) and besides we had no choice but to press on and hope the midwife arrived in time. Logic (as far as you can think clearly when in the final stages of labour) told me it was not a problem, I was not in danger. My baby arrived safely and luckily for us, so did the mid-wife, (unbrushed hair and teeth, still in her pyjamas) within minutes of the birth and so we had someone with the right gear to cut the umbilical cord. My husband had suggested going to the shed to get the garden shears to do those honours and it was whilst we were arguing over this that our saviour burst in with her medical bag. When the GP came around later that morning he asked why we hadn't called 999 when we realised I was not going to be able to get to hospital in time (and no I didn't have a short labour. I'd been in labour most of the night) to which I replied 'it was not an emergency'. I became more adept at dialling 999 as my child grew up, but at least his entry into the world was paramedic and siren free. Giving birth at home ended up being a lovely way to welcome a new child into our lives, and my husband, much to his embarrassment, acquired hero status and local notoriety for his role in the drama that spring day.

Anxiety with PTSD went it first started meant I thought everyone was going to die. I understood this to an extent. But I also developed anxieties unrelated to my trauma. I was worried about driving on the motorway and when I had no other choice, I could not drive in anything other than the inside lane, stuck between caravans and HGVs. I could not over-take cars, and often got stuck behind L-drivers, tractors and more caravans. It was exhausting; I'd grip the steering wheel for dear life and on a long journey that makes your hands ache. It made my journeys twice as long, as I drove slowly and avoided motorways as much as I could. Worse still, I found crossing the road a farce. I'd stand on the edge of the pavement and look left and right, over and over. I could not put my foot into the road to cross unless there was not a car in sight. This was tricky when working in London, Manchester, New York or Boston. My friends joked that if I stood on street corners for too long, I might get new business. On a business trip to New York as I was ultra-scared to cross the roads (as the rules are different state-side) I ended up grabbing my colleague's hand like a scared child. We laughed once we got to the other side and for the rest of the trip my colleague took my hand each time we crossed the street. I was glad to have such understanding colleagues. When the police called to our home about a bout of recent burglaries in our area, as soon as I saw the officer at the gate, I felt sick, my stomach turning over, my heart racing, my mouth dry, it took a hell of a lot of breathing to stop myself from passing out. I believed my son was dead. I was visibly shaking when I opened the door to the sergeant, so much so that his first words were reassuringly blurted out empathically, 'I didn't mean to scare you. Nothing bad has happened. Are you alright though?'

Anxiety made me feel very small, so very, very small; everyone and everything around me felt big, gigantic. It was like being a little beetle under the shadow of a large boot about to squash me flat; pressing the fight out of me, flattening my spirit, killing my courage, crushing the rational me.

Hiding

'I want to be invisible. I want to hide. I want to disappear.' Was this Me talking? For an extrovert the feeling of wanting to be unnoticed was alien, incongruous. I started to avoid people. It was one of the triggers that prevented me from being able to do my job. I could not cope going into the office to be with colleagues and clients. I could not handle the London Underground: I had terrible panic attacks every time I went into the City office until eventually, I stopped going into London on public transport altogether. I avoided crowded places. I thought twice about going to the cinema, only going in off-peak times when it was quiet. I found going at times when the OAP showing was on meant the cinema was almost empty. No-one ever asked me to prove my age. Not sure if I was offended or not by that, but sitting in an almost empty dark auditorium with the pensioners was peaceful.

I'd never experienced apathy and got cross when people had an attitude of 'can't be asked': but in my moments of flatness, I found myself thinking just that. Why bother'. This sentiment led to a spiral of self-loathing as I noticed my indifference. My brain was not being a good friend. I felt empty some days and found solace in withdrawing into myself; staying at home safe, reading, crying, listening to music and being alone. I was safe alone. I was safe if I stayed hidden; keeping away from people and stimuli. Besides it was easier to hide from people, it involved less energy; hiding meant I didn't have to pretend to be fine, I didn't have to put on my smile.

Keeping safe
Hiding
Being invisible
Keeping the world out
Staying home
Being quiet
Ignoring the world
Keeping safe, safe, hidden, safe

When I was around people, I often felt distant, like being in a bubble floating above the conversation and scene. I was as if there was a thin, invisible veil between me and any company. one that often manifest as me hearing but not listening, looking but not seeing and nodding but not understanding. It was like being on pause, seconds behind time, a fraction slower. Hidden in full sight. Hidden by an unseen curtain.

Numbness

It was especially hard to handle my PTSD when it impacted on the relationship between me and my husband. Following each traumatic episode with the asthma I felt drained and numb. The numbness is hard to describe: it was more than lack of feeling, more than being unresponsive; it was like being a stone, impervious. It wasn't that I was cold or frozen, this suggest being able to feel. I felt inert. It was like having a local anaesthetic injection at the dentist, that dull lack of sensation. I carried a heaviness of nothingness. I battened down my hatches to stay safe, safe inside myself.

I couldn't feel
I didn't want to feel
I didn't want sex
I didn't want physical intimacy
I didn't want to be touched
I could not give or receive pleasure
I was inert
I was isolated
I was dead to feeling
Feeling anything

I felt nothing
I felt numb

Sex for me (and many women) is as much mental as physical; my emotions could not be aroused; my mind was out of reach. I discussed this numbness openly with my husband but it was something he struggled to accept and understand. I felt so guilty; what sort of woman was I becoming? Frigid? A few of my women friends who'd suffered post-natal depression shared their experiences about lack of sex drive and desire in an effort to help me. Most of these women faced long term tensions and consequences in their relationships for not wanting sex. We all agreed we felt guilty, misunderstood, and distressed. Lack of sexual desire for any reason is best tackled as a couple; after all, 'It takes two to tango' as my mum used to say. I don't blame myself. I worked hard to tackle the issue and in time, slowly, very slowly, the numbness faded, but I think a great damage was done to my marriage.

Flashbacks & Nightmares, the Criminals of PTSD

It was only after eight months of scribbling did I feel ready to write about my flashbacks and nightmares. For a long time this bucket had one lonely paragraph, one thought parked:

> 'Thinking about the past is too painful. I can't do it. The past when it rears its head is real, it's like being back there again: the smells, sounds, racing chest, feeling sick, feeling overwhelmed with fear. I try to keep the past horrors blocked off, hidden. The past creeps back in the day as flashbacks, and at night in bad dreams and nightmares. The horrors of the asthma attacks are still real. So bloody, bloody real.'

I had my first flashback about ten days after my son had the second near fatal asthma attack. I was driving on the motorway on my way to work when suddenly I saw what felt like a film running before my eyes; running in the air between me and the windscreen. The scene—

the children's ward at the John Radcliff Hospital, my little boy is lying on his hospital bed, wires creeping from his body, monitors beeping away, his nebuliser hissing, the other children and babies fast asleep. Suddenly he clutches his chest and screams 'my heart hurts'. I hit the emergency button on the back wall and, in what seems like a split second, a crash team arrive. The team push me away, push my son down and begin CPR. He's had a cardiac arrest. Age eight. I feel sick. My heart is hurting and beating fast. Everything seems to happen in slow motion. The sounds become distant. I am in my head, screaming 'This can't be happening. My eight-year-old son can't be dying'. I stand fixed to the spot. I'm terrified. A nurse appears, she is my daughter's Girl Guide teacher, I know her, and she recognises me immediately. She realises it's my offspring they are saving. She reaches out to me as I fall into a black hole and faint. Then there is silence. I feel a pause in the pandemonium. A voice in the distance says 'we've got him back, he's back'. This was a weird and cruel déjà vu. As I'm driving panic rises in my body and I feel I'm dropping into the back hole. This was horrifying: I was still driving looking through the images to stay in the right lane. I was sweating. I was shaking. I was there again. My throat was dry. I pulled over on the hard shoulder. As the flashback faded away I was trembling, physically and mentally exhausted from a couple of seconds of horror relived.

A couple of days later I had a different flashback: this time I was running down a cream walled corridor, following a hospital trolley with my child on it, the medical team moving fast, the doors open as if by magic as we enter ITU. I follow even though my legs feel heavy. As we enter the darkness of PICU (paediatric intensive care unit) my youngest crashes with a respiratory arrest. I raise one foot, I try to step forward and, as if in slow motion, I pass out. I feel the black cloak of fear push me down. I'm falling into blackness. Falling. Fearful and falling. Déjà vu on steroids. I had this second flashback whilst talking to a colleague and again it was like a film running in the space between us. Apparently, I went as white as a sheet. I was trembling with the fear; my heart was pounding; my mouth was dry. I was back in PICU watching the doctors save my child.

Over the years as my son had more life-threatening asthma attacks, and our visits to PICU became many, I began to have a number of different flashbacks: always reflecting the critical moments before, during and after the crashes. The sights, sounds, and smells were vivid and the atmosphere of my fear and panic tangible. I never had a voice in my flashbacks. I heard other sounds, medical machines, body monitors, doctors and nurses' voices. My mouth would open but no sound came out. I was struck dumb with fear. It was like an out of body experience, I was there and yet not there, I was part of the pain, but also an observer. The flashbacks came at such random moments: when I was cooking dinner, reading a book, having fun at the theatre, out for a meal, or in a meeting at work. Each time I was left shaken and disturbed, it was an effort to conceal my distress. The flashbacks came at a rate of two or three a day to two or three a month; I never knew or worked out what triggered them. I learnt to breathe through them and let them pass.

During my therapy in 2019/20 I was asked to recall a memory, one flashback we could work with. This was extremely difficult; I had so many memories, so many flashbacks, all traumatic, all horrific, all overwhelming, and all very, very vivid. I settled on the first flashback as this one had caused me the most distress. Overtime I'd became tolerant and accepting of the flashbacks: I thought they were part of the course and that in time they would stop. But for two years each flashback was a new horror movie; nothing crueller than reality. I had flashbacks of my son crashing at home in my arms; having a heart attack while being loaded into an ambulance on my drive; and suffering respiratory arrests late at night in A&E.

The nightmares were as bad, if not worse: worse because I'd scream in my sleep. My screams were terrifying for my family. I could wake the house up with my distressing cries. On a camping trip I woke over fifty happy-campers as my chilling screams filled a Welsh field. The farmer thought someone was being murdered and was not far off dialling 999. My nightmares were a combination of reality and fiction segued visions of death; the death of my son. In my nightmares, 'we've got him back' became 'he's gone, he's dead'. This was usually the point of my screaming. Sometimes the devil got involved in my nightmares and followed me around threatening to take my children. The devil would tell me no matter how hard I worked to keep my children safe, no matter how many asthma action plans I wrote, no matter how religious I was about my son taking his medication, he would take him away from me. I don't believe in the devil but his appearance was a disturbing and terrifying presence in my nightmares. Sometimes I woke myself up with the screaming. I'd be shaking and sweating with distress. Other times I'd cry on and on until one of my children carefully coaxed me awake. It was upsetting for my children to witness my nightmares but I never told them the details. Nightmares are contagious so I kept the horror to myself. I'd be unsettled and on edge the days following the nightmares, as it had felt so real and I was tired from lack of decent sleep.

Guilt & Dissing Yourself

Guilt was my second skin. I wanted therapy to peel it away. Guilt according to Wikipedia:

Guilt is an **emotional experience** that occurs when a person believes or realizes—accurately or not—that they have compromised their own standards of conduct or have violated universal moral standards and **bear significant responsibility** for that violation.

Guilt and feeling shit about yourself. This was a whole new ball game for me. I'd never been one to waste time on putting myself down or feeling guilty for no good reason or even being anxious over my looks, weight, Welsh accent, height (or lack of). I had a lot to be proud of. When I started dissing myself (as the kids would say), I did it with all the energy, drive and passion that I did most things. I ended up hating myself, big time. I wrote this down as part of my diatribe to my GP to help him understand where I was at in my head:

> *"I'm hard work. I find living with me exhausting. I know I overthink things, but I cannot stop. I'm bored of this pain; I'm boring. I'm pathetic. I'm wasting so much by being un-me. It's all in my head. I want to switch my head off. I want to stop thinking. I want to stop feeling so sad, so bad, so scared, so pathetic, so weak and so wasteful (of life and time). I want to run away and hide. I hate myself, for being weak. I hate myself for being so nasty inside; I hate what I'm thinking. I'm a lie. I hate liars. I hate myself."*

I realised I'd been beating myself up, feeling weak because I couldn't cope and feeling (even though I knew it was quite irrational) to blame for the situation with my husband; thinking I should have done things differently. I shouldn't have thought I could solve his problem; I should have asked for help before. I'd been telling myself to buck up, stay in control, keep the negativity out. But it was not working. I felt pathetic. I blamed myself for not protecting my children from the pain, frustration and confusion of living with an alcoholic father. I felt guilty for going down the divorce route. I held myself responsible for the anxieties my children had to endure during my husband's year-long critical sickness with kidney disease. I saw myself as an arrogant failure. I had not been able to stay married, in sickness and health, for richer or poorer, to love and to cherish. I'd failed. I'd wanted to provide a loving home for my family till death do us part. I thought I'd married for life. I was determined to work to achieve that; I was not expecting it to be a bed of roses; after all I'd seen my parents fail the marriage exercise. I was dissing myself big time over failing.

I'd reason to call myself stupid as I started losing some of my key skills. I struggled with programs at work, and had issues remembering passwords. At work I constantly asked IT for help for the simplest of tasks. I was becoming a pain—No, I was a pain.

Guilty as charged.
Crime: not coping.

To-do List

For most of life I've lived by a simple set of rules:

Eat well.

Exercise often.

Make an effort.

As a working mum it was hard to exercise as often as I'd have liked, but for most of my adulthood I was able to stick to my rules. I do love a rule. I like to set them ambitious enough that I feel inspired to keep them but vague enough that I can't punish myself for not keeping to them. For example, eat well—what exactly does that mean? In my book, it means don't overeat, don't diet (Did I Eat That; four letter word), don't eat too many processed, sugary or fatty foods, and eat plenty fresh fruit and veg each day. Not a taxing rule but a great self-monitor, keeps you on the right side of the BMI index, just.

When I began suffering PTSD badly in 2019, I made a conscious decision to keep my rules. Gee, did I make an effort. I made a list of additional things to be done each day/week. I made the decision that these things were not negotiable, and there had to be a very good reason not to stick to the must-do list. Good reasons included the weather, physical sickness, family dilemmas, or a work crisis (this was pre-Covid-19).

Must-do list:
Get up every day as usual
Maintain self-care: shower, do hair, face on
Get Dressed
Dress nicely
Eat breakfast
Go to work or do whatever was on schedule for
    the day
Cook nice suppers
Eat at the table
Be kind to myself
Rest
Relax
Read
Walk 20 to 30 km a week
Keep house clean and tidy
Walk and talk with friends
Lunch with my girlfriends
Go to the theatre often

Keep the hobbies up—knitting, sewing, making jam
and chutney
Learn to garden (a necessity at the time, since my
husband and I had separated)

Not-to-do List

I can be a slave driver, more to myself than towards others, although my children and colleagues may disagree. My not-to-do list was as important as the to-do list.

Don't:
drink too much
give up
be afraid to cry
feel the need to be busy
be ashamed
let yourself go (as in become a slob)
wear track suit pants before 6pm or after 8.30am
skip meals
forget this list

Some may read this list and think 'what a saddo', 'how controlling' or at best, 'hey lady, learn to chill and go with the flow'. Throughout my journey with PTSD I did manage to keep to the rules, in the main, even when the Covid-19 pandemic broke out in early 2020. These rules helped me not so much because they were things I could control but more because they are good habits to adopt to stay healthy. I know these simple habits helped me keep my head above water. Despite drowning in fear and anxiety, these were rules not to be broken. If I could keep this effort up, just like doggy paddling, I knew I'd get to the shore or be rescued. I knew I had to keep myself physically strong to withstand the waves of despair.

Why did I persevere with these rules you may ask? Simply because I knew there was enough good quality research and evidence showing good diet, regular exercise, suitable rest and being involved in culture or hobbies are regenerative and essential for longer term well-being. I could not give up. I had to make an effort myself. I was sure I could rely on my own body to help me help myself. I hoped to stimulate my natural pain killers into doing their stuff. Enkephalins and endorphins to the rescue.

Asking for Help

Asking for help is important but when you're struggling it's easier said than done. More often than not it's impossible to do. You are lost, deep in the hole you can't see your pain, you can't put words to the problem, and you feel guilty. You feel a burden. I felt weak and undeserving of help. So, I kept quiet for a long time. Too long. Wonderful hindsight again.

And then there comes pride. I was too proud to ask for help. When my PTSD reared its ugly head in early 2019, I thought I could cope. Who can I ask for help? I struggled with that question.

> Who can I talk to?
> Who can I trust?
> Who will understand?
> Who will not judge me or laugh at me?
> Who will truly listen?

Truly listen and not tell me 'chin up' or 'chill'.

Why is it so hard to ask for help? For most of us, talking about mental health issues with others is difficult. Really difficult. Most books will tell you that the common fears among those considering getting help for mental illness include, rejection, embarrassment and misperception. I was most afraid of misperception. I thought others would see me as weak, self-absorbed or at worst, crazy. Mental health exists on a spectrum, but at the time I did not fully appreciate this. I did not know what to ask for help for. I knew I did not feel normal, normal for me; but did that mean I was sick? Did that mean I was crazy? Did that mean I needed help?

I believe it's critical that others have the sense, emotional antenna and confidence to step in:

To reach out
To probe
To offer an ear
To watch
To protect
Even to take control in some cases

Signals, emotional antenna, instinct, intuition, sensitive, call it what you like, look for the signs, they will be there. People rarely suffer in silence; the signs and signals will be there. I beg you to look for them and acknowledge them, in yourselves and others. If you are self-aware you may know what your stress signs are; and it's a good idea to tell others what to look out for. Give them licence to step in when your signals are flashing. My signals of distress include being OTT, going into overdrive with doing things, achieving things, taking on more, working harder, cleaning more and being short tempered with those not pulling their weight. I'm hyper critical of others but over sensitive to criticism of me. I'd shared this insight with my colleagues giving them authority to help me help myself. Thankfully for me one of my HR colleagues did listen and had the guts to step in and take control when I was falling into the pit of PTSD. I will admit I still find it hard to ask for help. My default setting is COPE. I told my family and friends to find a way in, to observe, be vigilant and if necessary, take control (for a while). Don't wait for me to ask. By the time I ask, I'm in deep waters. Please reach out to those whose pain and distress you see or feel, however subtle the signs. Be the person who asks 'are you ok?'. But don't move on when you get the answer, 'I'm fine mate', 'ok', 'not too bad'. Ask again, 'really ok?' and wait. If you wait, I bet you the answer will be different. Asking twice opens the door to a real dialogue. It could be the conversation that saves someone, that helps them get it out. I have always felt repeating yourself is a good thing. Try it.

Getting Help

It is early autumn 2019, and I don't yet know PTSD is the problem. I only know I'm not right. I'm not the usual me, I'm not coping, and I can't do much more to help myself. I'm talking openly, walking miles each day, cooking great new vegan meals, drinking much less Chardonnay, going to the theatre, reading uplifting books and I'm keeping in regular touch with my friends and children. I'm not giving in. I'm not going to slide into a black hole, or take antidepressants. I'm off sick. I'm not at work. I'm not in control of my life as I want and need to be. At the moment.

I don't believe depression is the issue. Yes, I've symptoms of depression (new in itself for me). I know there are some days I don't want to get out of bed or leave the house and I'm scared of meeting people. I have symptoms of depression and anxiety, I admit that. At work, I've hidden in the toilets too scared to face colleagues or clients. But I never, ever gave in to those feelings at work. I carried on. I forced myself to act normal. Even now while I'm off work, I'm able to get up, wash, and dress well and force myself to face the world. I keep to my routine. I make an effort, a lot of effort, and the mere fact I can must mean depression is not the causative issue. I've seen and talked to people who can't make the effort work; they have lost the capacity to try. The depression label does not sit easily with me, not because I'm ashamed to be depressed, but because I know the right label/diagnosis matters if I'm to get the right help. I can still feel happy, I still try. I try very hard. Plenty of things make me smile and laugh. I feel I've too much energy and emotion for a diagnosis of depression.

October 2019, back home in the UK after a trip to Jordan, signed off sick. Struggling with what I know include *some* symptoms of depression and anxiety.

I discuss with my GP the extent of my disabling negative feelings. I insist I'm not depressed per se. What can be wrong? I'm walking miles each day, doing mindfulness, reading uplifting books, walking and talking with friends, doing lunch, going vegan, not drinking alcohol, and making curtains for my boy's new home. I'm busy and working hard to drive out the negative shit. But I'm bored of listening to myself. I'm bored to trying to understand what is happening to me. I could scream with frustration. It takes so much effort to keep smiling and appear to cope. The incongruous thing is I'm looking better than I've done for a while. The fresh air, exercise and new vegan diet mean I've lost weight and my skin is looking rosy. But inside it's ugly and dark.

I remained convinced I didn't have depression. I believed this with some caution; I know depression can disable the best of people. My mum suffered badly in her later years, understandably as she was failing in health and also very lonely. But people with depression don't have the energy I have, people with depression are isolated, people with depression can't hide it, can't help themselves; they struggle with self-care. Depression definitions according to Me; all misguided, I was terribly mistaken; showing my ignorance and arrogance.

When talking about my mental state, I sounded sane, rational, and extremely self-aware. But in talking I was filtering, ordering and rationalising my emotions. To help my GP understand how ugly, scared and desperate I felt inside, I wrote down ten pages of painfully honest diatribe. It was a rant with no holds barred. Once I'd emptied myself of the agony, I couldn't read it back. I typed it out and put it straight in an envelope before I could change my mind. On reading the diatribe my GP and I agree I'd benefit from getting some specialist help. We agreed to find a counsellor who would be skilled and specialist enough to provide me with cognitive behavioural therapy (CBT). I admit I was reluctant about going down the CBT and counsellor route due to a poor experience

ten years before when I first had problems with flashbacks
and bad memories as part of PTSD.

I am sick
I need to get better
I am weak
I need to get stronger
I am hurting
I need to be healed
I am scared
I need protection
I am lonely
I need a friend
I am going insane
I need someone to listen
I am sinking
I need support
I am drowning
Please reach for me

The Right Therapist

As the years passed the terror of those memories and the fear that my son would die, gradually faded. Certainly, because he appeared to have grown out of the severe asthma, I believed we had all healed. How wrong I was. Little did I know my head had not been processing my horrific memories in the right part of my brain? My memories were badly parked.

So, in 2005 against a backdrop of flashbacks and nightmares I agreed to see a therapist for help. First consultation was to share my symptoms with a brief overview of why I was there—in essence a summary of the traumatic events I'd witnessed with the asthma attacks. Second consultation covered what was I doing to help myself. I ticked all the right boxes: exercise, talking, resting when these events tired me out and not too much chardonnay. I got that I had PTSD. I understood this was my mind responding to trauma. I believed I'd come through this. I just needed the therapist to show me how; give the advice, skills, support and understanding to guide me through. Sadly, on this occasion my expectations were not met.

In the third session I was telling the therapist why my finger was bandaged up. Over the weekend I'd had friends around for a BBQ. I was busy chopping the salad, talking excitedly and stupidly sliced into one of my fingers. A clean slice as my husband had not long sharpened our good quality knives. The story I was telling was amusing: husbands being cave men around BBQ, thinking they were doing the cooking as they poke a sausage. Kids going OTT on the trampoline, too many on there for safety but they were having fun so why spoil it; the wives trying to fit all the food on the table and make sure the kids didn't knock drinks over as they ran in and out of the kitchen. 'Picture me' I say to the counsellor 'telling my story when I badly slice through my finger in close vicinity of my friend who usually faints at the sight of blood'. I quickly bound my finger up the best I could, not wanting to distress my friend, alarm my guests and have my husband remind me not to use the newly sharpened knives. Later that night when our guests were gone, realising my finger was throbbing and swelling, we removed the too tight dressing to release an alarmingly deep cut. My finger restarted bleeding copiously and we ended up going to the local minor injuries unit to get my finger stitched, and left with a precautionary dose of antibiotics. Moral of my story, lesson learnt; be careful with sharp knives and no talking while cutting lettuce.

Once the amusing story was told to the therapist I was expecting to get onto the flashbacks and dreams that were troubling me; but the therapist appeared fixated with the knives story. She kept asking me what was my problem with knives, why were knives such a problem for me? Why had I used such a sharp knife to cut salad if I'd known it was dangerous? I was confused and at first, I thought this was a joke. I asked could we move off the subject of knives and onto my more pressing problems but this made the therapist convinced I had a knives problem or I was hiding something more sinister. I felt misunderstood and as if I was in an absurd Monty Python's Flying Circus sketch. I got up, declared the session was not working, that I was done with therapy and left, vowing to never to see a therapist again.

Coming back to 2019 and the agreement I'd made with HR about seeking help. Since my last experience with a therapist over fifteen years before, things had really moved on in terms of awareness of mental health. Initiatives such as annual Mental Health Awareness months, weeks and days and in the UK, government driven policy and research had recognised the impact of mental health on the one in four individuals who suffer each year. High profile people were speaking of their mental health struggles and the sad suicides of people well known in the media appeared to be taking the stigma out of 'being crazy', 'going mad' or 'losing the plot'.

I found asking for help and actually getting the right help two very separate things. Timing is critical to getting suitable help. Despite all the awareness, it seemed the services to help people such as me were not keeping up:

I was not suicidal,
I was not self-harming,
I was not drinking excessively,
I was not doing drugs,
I was able to look after myself,
I was in employment,
I was not a danger to myself or others.

I got up each day and washed and dressed; I ate well and I walked miles each week. It appeared I was functioning quite normally. In discussion with my GP about where to get the help and how quickly I could be seen, it seemed it would be sometime (months) before I could be seen within the NHS. I was fortunate to have private health cover through my job and it made sense to take that route. I made contact with my health cover provider who quite promptly assessed my claim. This was my first experience of being formally assessed for mental well-being. Through a series of questions (over the phone) relating to how I felt, the frequency and strength of a series of negative symptoms and the impact on my daily activities, the person on the end of the telephone came to the conclusion I did need help. My provider discussed some practicalities in terms of how far would I travel to see a therapist and would I prefer a male or female and time of day. It's important you think about these practicalities, as initially you are confiding in a complete stranger. Only you know who you will feel comfortable talking to. The travel to and from a therapist needs to be carefully considered as the sessions may upset or disturb. Consideration of being escorted with a friend is valid. Timing is important, the sessions need to work for your personal life and also when you are most receptive. I am a morning person and thus chose to have my sessions at midday, leaving me ample (cos I worry about being late) time to travel, park and get a hot chocolate before the can of worms would be opened. I imagined going private would mean I'd be seen quickly, say a week or two. But with the high demand for therapists even I had to wait some weeks; during that time my first choice for a very local (five miles away) person would have meant an eight-week wait and so I opted for therapist in my nearest city, fifteen miles away. I was eligible under my policy for eight sessions, thus, I worked out, I could have the problem sorted by Christmas. Or so I thought. Ever one to set objectives. Always one to drive for an expedited solution. No time to waste. I needed the old Me back.

Diagnosis

It's important to get the right diagnosis if you want to be successful in managing, relieving or curing any illness. It was this rational that fuelled my belief that I was not suffering from depression in 2019. Getting the right label, the right diagnosis was the only way I was going to get the right help. When I first spoke to a therapist in late 2019, I was adamant—'I do not have depression'. When I reflect back it sounds arrogant and ignorant. However, I admitted to her I had symptoms that included depression and anxiety, but also a hell of a lot more negative and disabling emotions. The dark new emotions for me included fear, anger, pain, misery, hopelessness, sadness, and indecision. I had no vision for the future, and I was scared, really truly scared. At my first appointment I was prepared. I knew I'd need to describe my symptoms, mention how they impact my daily life and probably define what I wanted to achieve from therapy; I'd need to give an overview of what was going on in my life that was possibly the root of the problem; I was ready for tears, knowing this was going to be like opening a wound or pressing on a bad bruise. There was going to be no way I could hold back my emotions; I was nervous, I'd ramble on and blurt everything out incoherently. I was ready for all of this. I decided to not to write anything down prior to my appointment. I didn't want to predict the course of this help. I wanted to learn to step back and allow the experts to guide me. I wanted to be open. I wanted to listen. After all, one of my current problems was I was no longer able to make decisions, any decisions. My way of doing things had not worked to date. Best go into the therapy room empty handed, one receptive Me.

I blurted out so much in my first session. I talked fast, wanting to get all the background stuff out so we could press on with the treatment ASAP. I managed to precis my last twenty years into 15 minutes. I reiterated that I didn't think I had depression per se. I was arrogant enough to say that I knew what the part of the problem was. I recall saying, 'Over the last 15 years I've joked that, in response to a number of awful constant life events, I will schedule a nervous breakdown. It feels like I am having that breakdown now. Only thing is, it's not funny. I know what the problem is, my brain has got stuck, stuck responding to danger; I'm in fight-flight-freeze mode all the time. I'm shit scared all the time. I feel in battle constantly. I'm at war with my head. I walk around with this black hole on my left shoulder. I'm on the edge of the black hole and dangerously close to falling in, hanging on by my fingertips. The slightest thing can make me feel like I'm slipping into the blackness. I'm doing everything I can to stay out of that hole. I'm working hard to stay in control, to understand what is happening to me and doing what I can to move myself from the edge. I'm working hard to get back to being me, the person who never loses the plot or gives in, never lets you down; the person you can rely on to solve problems, who can shovel the shit and still smile.

The happy Me.
The positive Me.
The coping Me.
Where is she?

I'm scared. I am living with so much bloody fear. I am frightened most of the time—No—correction, all of the time—24-7. I'm terrified of such mundane things.

Scared,
frightened,
anxious,
panicky,
hyper,
and angry,
so bloody angry.

I am hiding all this, compartmentalising it is exhausting. I can't think clearly, can't focus or concentrate. I have to work hard to stop myself from bursting, screaming, or worse still, running away to hide. I want to be invisible. I want this pain to stop. I'm like a tightly set trap, ready to spring at a feather's touch. Spring into dread—dread of things going wrong; I dread the death of those close to me.

The first step to getting the right help for any medical problem is to know what you are dealing with. An accurate diagnosis can often take time and in many clinical areas involve lots of tests and consultations. Clinical teams will be interested to know what your symptoms are and how long you have had them and how they impact your daily life. A blood test can confirm if you have diabetes, and an X-ray can identify broken bones; for most mental health concerns there are no medical test to rule a condition in or out; there are no categorical tests to measure your mind. Medical teams get a handle of your mental state by talking to you and asking you very specific questions. Rarely do they perform brain scans or take blood tests. I was ready to answer the questions honestly, as at the time there were so many normal things I was unable to do; like going out, talking to people, going into supermarkets and crowded places. I could not do these things because I was:

Scared	so, so scared
Anxious	so bloody anxious
Edgy	irritatingly twitchy
Angry	unbelievable mad inside
Numb	so dead flat emotionally
Empty	all washed up

I lost track of time in the first session and before time was up, I was asked to complete a questionnaire. I did not know it at the time but it was a questionnaire that would clarify if I had PTSD. The questions were designed to measure the effect of routine life stress, everyday traumas and acute stress. I came to learn the questionnaire was called The Impact of Event Scale—Revised (IES-R).

The IES-R was designed as a measure of PTSD symptoms in adults, and is a short, easily administered self-report questionnaire. It can be used for repeated measurements over time to monitor progress. The questionnaire has 22 questions. There are three areas the questions look at: intrusion which covers intrusive thoughts, nightmares, intrusive feelings and imagery, and dissociative-like re-experiencing; avoidance which covers numbing of responsiveness, avoidance of feelings, situations, and ideas; and thirdly hyperarousal which covers anger, irritability, hypervigilance, difficulty concentrating, heightened startle. Once all the questions are answered the scores are tallied up and the results consist of a total raw IES-R score, and raw scores for three subscales: the Avoidance Scale, Intrusion Scale, and the Hyperarousal Scale.

The questions are simple and all you have to do is score each one on a scale of 0 to 4 for level of distress, from 0 not at all, 1 a little bit, 2 moderately, 3 quite a bit, 4 extremely distressed. The questions are specific to a life event that you identify and you score the distress over a defined period, usually the last week or month. The questions cover trouble staying asleep, concentrating and avoiding thinking about the life event and having dreams about it. I filled the questionnaire in quickly and was aware I was scoring most questions as 3 or 4. There was only one question I scored 0; I felt as if it hadn't happened or it wasn't real. The trauma of those asthma attacks was always real, really, really real.

Unfinished Business

At the second consultation with my therapist, she confirmed I had PTSD. The results from the questionnaire I had completed at my first consultation suggesting I really did need help before PTSD impacted my health further. The questionnaire had identified that I fell into the category 'PTSD with a high enough score to suppress my immune system's functioning (even 10 years after an impact event).' That was a shock, but as soon as the words 'Post Traumatic Stress Disorder' were said it all made sense. I know it sounds odd, why I would feel relief to have PTSD. I was relieved because I knew this enemy; we had crossed paths before; we had unfinished business. My PTSD, my Fear, my Coping, my Dread.

But what does this mean now? Why hadn't I spotted that the PTSD was back? The answer was that I had crammed the PTSD into one of my compartments. I had been operating in survival mode for years. Surviving had become my norm. My PTSD was not going to stay hidden any more. I was going to do more than survive. I wanted to thrive.

PTSD

Painful	Personal
Terrifying	Toxic
Sad	Silent
Dread-full	Disabling

FEAR

Failure

Encompassing

Abnormal

Reality

COPE

Can't

Overwhelming

Pathetic

Empty

DREAD

Doom

Repeating

Envelops

Agony

Dark

It's Not All in the Mind

It was sometime before I realised it was not only my brain that was acting up. Around the time I began hiding in the toilets and crying for no reason (February 2019), I started getting acute pain on my right side. It came and went and eventually I noticed it was worse after eating and gave me most jip at night. I had no other symptoms so initially I didn't worry; I'd recently had an over 50's MOT and bowel cancer screen, and passing both with flying colours. However, after three months I mentioned the pain to my GP and he ran some tests to rule out anything sinister. Once the tests came back normal, we agreed the pain was most likely IBS. I left the surgery with advice for managing IBS and a prescription. I know quite a bit about IBS, my daughter having suffered terribly over the years. My daughter thinks of the gut as our 2nd brain and there is some science behind this, with researchers having shown that fat cells in the stomach have four times more cortisol receptors than elsewhere in the body. I'd never had gut problems before (expect for acute appendicitis and the odd bout of food poisoning), but I began to realise my body was under stress with the IBS yet another signal I was not 100%; I needed to consider these symptoms as part of my overall well-being. Easy enough to say, but how was I going to manage the IBS alongside my mental health, a new problem. If I sorted my mental health out, I was convinced my gut would follow suit. But after a few months of acute crippling episodes of IBS pain, I accepted a prescription medicine to help, and it made a big difference when the attacks kicked off.

Towards the mid-year point of 2019 one of my old problems had raised its ugly head, Lichen Planus. Lichen Planus is an autoimmune condition of the skin and mouth, seen mainly in the over 40s and more common in women. Basically, I had a very sore mouth. The inside of my cheeks was covered with solid misty white patches, the extent of the whitewash ran to the back of my mouth and along the underside of my tongue. It looked like I had natural yogurt painted on my inner cheeks. My cheeks and tongue were red, swollen and chewed up. I could see teeth marks on the flesh of my cheeks. I knew what this problem was having had it on and off since I was forty, in fact it started not long after my son was in admitted to intensive care with his first near fatal asthma attack. I continued to have symptoms on and off over the decade he was sick, and later on as other stressful life events became part of my reality. But this time around the symptoms were awful, my mouth was sore and eating was difficult and uncomfortable. Rather than moan, or suffer in silence I saw my dentist and GP both of whom agreed my mouth was a mess and it made sense to seek expert advice. I was fortunate to see an oral surgeon relatively quickly courtesy of my private health insurance. The surgeon was on the ball and after a whistle-stop summary of my health and personal situation, and my previous history of Lichen Planus, he considered me holistically. I was reassured there were no sinister signs of oral cancer, and not having Lichen Planus in other more delicate private orifices meant I'd no reason to worry too much. The surgeon explained the medication I'd been prescribed to help my PTSD symptoms can cause some people to clench their jaw or grind their teeth. I'd no evidence of teeth grinding but certainly of jaw clenching (bruxism.). Was this chicken or egg, catch 22? Was the medication part of the problem, or the PTSD the main culprit? More to the point, how was I going to manage this new problem? We agreed it made sense to get to the bottom of my mental health (once again sort the health of my head out and my mouth would follow) and in the meantime get a gum shield to wear at night. The main objective now was to reduce aggravating the Lichen Planus by the bruxism. A gum shield was secured through my dentist, tailor made, fitting like a glove. Early signs are that the night time plastic smile is working, with my cheeks looking less like the dregs of an old trifle.

Fear, pain, sadness, anxiety and emptiness hurt in so many places. The hurt is real and I feel it in my head, my heart and that part of me I consider my soul. The hurt is also tangible and physical; my gut (IBS) and my mouth (Lichen Planus) proof enough. The IBS and Lichen Planus are still with me and they are my yard stick by which I measure my recovery and mental health. When they appear, I know to be more mindful, careful and kind to myself.

Talking About Stress……

When I first started talking about my emotions, I used language I was used to. I was clinical, objective and factual, avoiding vocabulary that had any hint of self-pity or weakness. I tried not to overdramatise or exaggerate, incongruous as it sounds for one who really loves a good dose of hyperbole in a story. I tried to come across as in control, level headed and rational. I detected that this way of communicating was to my detriment; people were struggling to see I was in serious distress. It was during the process of securing a therapist I realised how specific my language needed to be. I recall distinctly the questions the triage nurse asked me during a telephone assessment. As we moved through the questions, I sensed I was giving the impression of someone functioning normally. I was getting up, showing up, getting dressed, eating regularly, etcetera, etcetera, etcetera. I appeared to be someone who had no need of therapy. I wanted to scream at the nurse 'I'm doing all the right things, walking bloody miles, eating the right food, not drinking, talking to friends till I'm bored to death, but I am still drowning in a sea of agony. I am bored, so bloody bored of myself. I need help'.

At the time the questioning that irked me were those

around suicide: did I have suicidal thoughts, had I wanted to kill myself, did I think things would be better if I was dead? My answers to all these questions were no. An absolute, definitive no; no, I want to live. I don't want to be dead; I want to be strong. I want to be Me again. I know what it feels like to want to be dead: I had tried to take my own life twice when I was fifteen, slitting my wrist and a paracetamol overdose. At fifteen I didn't actually want to be dead; I just wanted all the pain to stop. I wanted to feel nothing, to be invisible. I wanted to run away and not be me anymore. I know that the space between not wanting to feel anymore and wanting to be dead is unbelievably narrow, it's a sliver of a slip from wanting to be invisible to making it all stop by taking your own life. I know because that is how I felt at fifteen, but here and now I just want to be back to being the coping Me. I wanted my life back so badly.

I also struggled with the questions on stress. Stress is over used as an all-encompassing term.

Stress
Pressure
Strain
Hassle
Life

There is no medical definition of stress. Health care professionals themselves disagree over whether stress is the cause of problems or the result of them. I couldn't readily answer the questions the triage nurse asked me about stress. I see stress as a normal part of work. I expect to be under pressure, I expect change, and when all is said and done, I was well paid to deal with trouble in my job. I'm happy, and expect, to carry a certain level of stress both at home and at work, I view it as part and parcel of life. My problem was not that I was stressed, but that I could not do my job, i.e. I could not do stress, a subtle but critical difference.

I was distressed

Rather than just answer the questions, I exploded with frustration and anxiety, crying and explaining how scared, lonely and angry I was; how I could not cope. Pain in public, burden off loaded, getting it out. After the outburst the triage nurse agreed I needed help. At that point I cried uncontrollably, someone was listening and understanding. I came off the phone and cried for the rest of the day. Someone had heard me. I'd taken a step in the right direction.

Language, & Bad Language

I'm acutely aware that the vocabulary in my story is violent and sometimes I see alarm in people's faces when I talk to them. My conversation thermometer often reaches boiling point. I worry that if I carry on frightening people, I will be alone and abandoned. I swear more; I've never been prone to bad language, never needed to. I'm a talkative person and have ample vocabulary and gesticulation to get my messages across. Other people noticed my swearing more; this became a bit of a problem and embarrassment at work. I work with intelligent, well mannered, highly educated, nicely spoken people. We don't need to swear to do our jobs. So, when I started using vulgar language it was incongruous. It's not okay to say 'that's a shit plan', 'whose bloody idea is that?', 'have you got the balls to talk to the client about the problem?' or 'if you implement that strategy you'll be pissing in the wind'. I caught myself most times and apologised to my colleagues but I still cringe when I think back. I pride myself on having enough language skill to manage all situations without the need for profanities. I had two children, both with no pain relief, not even gas and air, and swore not even then. I'm not going to apologise for the bad and crude language I use in my PTSD journey. When I speak, I can tell you it's far worse. The violent language is a reflection of my head space; it's my head talking freely. I will not filter it; I will not stifle it. I have to listen to it. Words are powerful. I know they mean something. I have to be specific. I have to use the right words. I have to get it all out, no matter how distasteful, shocking or uncomfortable.

When talking about PTSD, I don't want to use language that suggests fighting. When I had melanoma, I couldn't relate to the idea of 'war on cancer'. War does harm, causes damage, fighting usually does, even in the playground. I admit I'm in turmoil; even if I consider PTSD my enemy, I'm better off negotiating. I will engage with my fear and anxiety and listen to their voices, hear them out. I will understand their perspectives and recognise, however unreasonable the demands of PTSD. If I ignore it, the fear will shout louder as the ignored tend to do. I will turn and acknowledge, deal with it, once and for all. I will make a peace treaty with my fear. There is a way forward without fear dominating my life.

CBT—Getting It Out—Talking About It

CBT or Cognitive Behavioural Therapy is a type of talking therapy. Talking therapies are psychological treatments to help people with mental and emotional problems. The therapy is provided by trained therapists who decide what type of therapy fits the problem and the person. Since writing this bucket I've learnt you don't need a referral from a GP to access this help on the NHS in England. But there is a snag; you need to be registered with a GP to access the support.

I'd agreed with my GP and HR director I'd get some CBT, and as mentioned in my bucket, 'The Right Therapist,' I ended up seeing a therapist through my employer-based private health insurance. By the time I was starting CBT it was October 2019 and I'd been suffering the symptoms of my distress (PTSD) acutely for nine months, and signed off from work for 6 weeks. Before starting CBT I was aware it was a pragmatic and highly structured way of addressing problems. I love structure and thus felt comfortable with the concept. I also liked the idea of the collaborative nature of the therapy, in that

I knew I'd be expected to agree with the therapist how to address the problem. I'd be the master of my destiny, I had to put the work in, and I'd have to make the effort. No good therapist would tell me what to do. I had to find my answers. To do that I'd have to feel, I'd have to be open and honest. I was sure I could manage that. I was desperate for help and I'd no intention of hiding anything. Trouble was, in my naivety, I'd no idea what was truly hidden away in my head. I didn't know I'd buried some feelings so deep they were invisible to me. CBT sells itself as a psychological treatment that focuses on current problems and it's mainly concerned with how we think and act now rather than attempting to resolve past issues. This was a hard concept for me as I was acutely aware that how I thought and thus acted was based on at least a decade of practice. How could I undo ten years of thinking the way I did, ten years of acting the way I did? How could I undo ten years of putting the bad feelings into the money box?

My therapist helped me understand that CBT would help me deal with the overwhelming nature of my feelings by breaking them down into smaller parts. I loved this idea; this is how I tackle problems, 'digestible chunks' as I say to my colleagues or family, 'start with bite size pieces, one step at a time, make it manageable'. During CBT my problems were looked at from five aspects:

My situation
My thoughts
My emotions
My physical feelings
My actions

CBT is based on the concept that these five aspects are interconnected and affect each other, such that my thoughts about a certain situation will affect how I feel both physically and emotionally, and thus influence how I act in response. I got that. It made sense when explained that way and I was given a super handout to help me understand the mechanics of this feedback loop. Roll on CBT I thought, I can do this. I believed I'd be back to normal by Christmas. But as we all know, easier said than done. The devil was in the detail and for me the hardest part was the separation out of my thoughts, emotions and physical feeling. I could identify the situation most accurately and analytically, no problem there. I always had to the ready a list of actions or options to address the situation. But the middle bits, oops, err, I got stuck. I had a well-worn route, a great short cut from situation (problem) to action (solution). Even if I did a little thinking it was clinical and I definitely ruled out emotions (these were dangerous things). Emotions cloud your judgement; they get in the way of solutions. No time to feel: what is the point of that? The result was that CBT for me was truly hard work and if it was not for the patience and persistence of my therapist to stick to the structure and keep me on track, I'd still be in the bottom of my black hole, stuck in my dark, ugly space.

I can talk once I get going, I really can; blame that Welsh gift of the gab. I tend to order, analyse and filter my dialogue either to provide context or information or just to make someone laugh. I don't bore people with detail and although I interrupt others, I'm irritated if I'm put off my conversation flow. I can't help but talk in stories to make a point. I talk for a reason. I realise when I talk, I want people to feel what I feel, see what I see, be there with me. I'm passionate, with gesticulation and mimicry all part of the storytelling. I understood I had to follow the rules of CBT; I had to cover the thoughts, emotions and feeling with as much energy and detail as any other conversation. I had to go into the darker places and find those negative feelings and describe them for my therapist with total honesty. After all there was a point to all this talking; it was to be my route back to normality.

I was going to give CBT a jolly good shot; I was going to give it all I had left. I slowly learnt that my thoughts, emotions and feelings were not facts. It was impossible to prove them, test them, reproduce them, but nonetheless they were my reality. During CBT I was never made to think of my thoughts, emotions or feelings as right or wrong. I learnt to accept them as a state of mind. However, I did consider my actions as facts. My actions could not be disputed:

I cried.
I dithered.
I hid in the toilets.
I avoided driving on the motorway.
I worked harder.
I stopped work.

During CBT my language exposed that I was thinking of myself in terms of two parts. The old Me was strong and coping. The sick Me is weak, pathetic and scared. This way of thinking wasn't helpful; following the CBT I began to think of myself as evolving, living and reshaping. I slowly, oh so very slowly, began to think, 'I am still me'. I understood, I felt 'I am still here'. I thought 'I am not lost'. Felt stronger little by little. I began to think, 'out the other side of this I will be different, not any less strong or any weaker, but reshaped. Evolution means survival of the fittest. I will do more than survive. I will thrive. I just need patience and time to develop self-compassion.'

CBT was like opening a Pandora's box, all my darkest secrets and memories flying into the open. My anguish, anger, frustration, dread, pain, sickness, despair, fear and loneliness, exposed. I had to learn to feel and accept these negative emotions; this was excruciatingly difficult. I had no tolerance of distress. I'd learnt since a child to block out hurtful emotions. I had a great knack and skill of shutting off anguish and misery. I'd honed these skills to an art once my youngest started having life threatening asthma attacks. I'd never let life's shit get me down. I didn't expect an easy ride through life; I was prepared and resilient. I was able to separate off the painful emotions and pop them in that money box. It worked for so long. But now the money box was full, smashed and the way CBT helped was in my acknowledgement of these feelings, this distress. Emotional distress is impossible to eliminate, its part and parcel of being human. Through CBT I had to learn to tolerate negative emotions. I had to understand why I believed these emotions to be a bad thing. I knew the answer to that straight off: I believed negative emotions were a waste of time; negative feelings were not helpful to implementing solutions. I believed these emotions meant I was weak and hinder my ability to cope. I'd had a lot to cope with from age seven to fifty-seven and I believed if I'd given in to these undesirable emotions I'd not be where I am today. I 'd never had anyone to turn to as a child; as the eldest of three children in a home where our parents were battling their way to a messy divorce, I learnt to cry silently. I learnt to cope alone. As a married woman and mother, I struggled to keep on top of my job, my home, my responsibilities and my sanity with sick children, my own health problems which included malignant melanoma whilst pregnant, and living with an alcoholic husband. I coped alone, again. There really was no time to feel. Believe me.

CBT helped me understand that my distress was associated with an inability of my brain to kick into my body's natural soothing system. There is science behind this concept and more to the point it made sense to me in that it reflected the way I behaved. I'd unconsciously shut off the gateway between my soothing system and my drive and threat systems. I'd never felt safe. I'd never felt protected. I only ever felt exposed, threatened and responsible. I had a strong desire, need, wish, ambition and drive to give my family all the protection, care and safe haven I'd been denied as a child and young adult. But

I could not see that unless I was truly safe, content and at harmony with my feelings I'd be unable to sustain my way of coping. I had to learn to sooth myself.

There were days my feelings were too much to bear. However, the CBT had provided me with the skills and tools to manage the negative shit when things became overwhelming. I'd shake when I felt fear and dread, truly shake. I felt sick, physically sick when I felt anxious; my heart raced when I felt panic stricken; I felt faint when I had flashbacks; my blood boiled when I felt angry and I stared into space for hours when I felt numb. I was disabled by these emotions and at this time I felt ashamed of myself for this. Adjusting my distress-intolerant beliefs was hard work as I've laboured on about, and I worked through six modules in addition to the weekly sessions with my therapist. I did the homework at my pace; some days it was a breeze and other days a slog. I found the most useful help was the question, 'If a friend held the same distress-intolerant belief for themselves, what advice would I give to them?' This helped me acknowledge the distress, put it in context and define the limits of its impact and define a new belief to hold about the distress. Basically, I'd talk to myself about myself. It helped. Best done in private or people get confused and think you are talking to them about problems they don't have. Even now I carry that question with me, with the additional one, 'What am I going to think and do differently?' For a start, I'm not ashamed anymore of my emotions or how I respond to them. That's progress. Believe me.

One of the tools that provided immediate relief when I was most crippled by my flashbacks and fear moments was Grounding. I had a vague idea about what the purpose of Grounding was, as I'd tried it occasionally when troubled the first time around with PTSD. However, I thought the technique quite lightweight and somewhat of a cosmetic solution, only covering over the canvass of horror. Initially I didn't hold out much hope it would help me in my times of acute distress. But with practice it did and in time it lessened the run-time of my flashbacks. Grounding techniques often use the five senses: sound, touch, smell, taste, and sight, to connect you with the present, diverting your attention from upsetting feelings. There are many suggestions for Grounding out there; my therapist gave me a list of 30 ideas and I did try them all. It was a painstaking process and I became very impatient, but in the end I found grounding techniques that worked for me. If I brushed my hair much like my nana used to do when I was little, I found that helped. Smelling herbs from my garden by rubbing the leaves of rosemary, thyme, sage, mint and lavender between my hands also calmed my brain. Looking at old photograph albums helped as it invariably made me laugh out loud; especially the photos of my university days with all the bad fashion and permed hair of the 1980s, or my children's parties with dozens of kids in dressing up gear (or no clothes at all in some toddler paddling pool parties) who are now mature sensible adults. If I was out and about and these options were not possible, I'd recite, either out loud or under my breath, the days of the week in Welsh. This required quite a concerted level of concentration as I'd not used my Welsh since being in school over 40 years ago. Starting with Dydd Llun (Deeth leen—Monday), I recited over and over again, in my natural West Walian lilt:

Dydd Llun
Dydd Mawrth
Dydd Mercher
Dydd Iau
Dydd Gwener
Dydd Sadwrn
Dydd Sul

If this did not work, I resorted, with hwyl, to the months of the year, either in Welsh or French, whatever my memory could handle at the time. You may wonder what hwyl (really put your lips together and pronounce as hoo-il) means; it does not translate directly from Welsh into English but is about feelings: those of power, passion, commitment all unseen, a deep inner positive vibe; putting your guts into it, elbow grease, as my nana would say.

I've worked in the life sciences all my life and spent my days dealing with clinical data, medical evidence and quantifiable facts. Most of the time the facts are not debatable: an answer is either right or wrong. I had to remind myself my feelings were not facts, but neither could they be debated. My feelings were my reality. My feelings were real and valid. They were not right or wrong, they just were. Fact. In the early days the CBT tools helped half of the time and with practice, and hywl, more so. I had six sessions of CBT and without them I'd not have been able to progress. CBT involved a lot of thinking, talking, and creative exploring of responses. I learnt a lot about distress intolerance and different ways to deal with negative emotions and situations. CBT helped me think very differently about distress and negative emotions; it helped me reframe them. It helped me look at negative emotions with a new perspective and appreciate their value and role (in the right context). CBT certainly, without any doubt, diminished my distress: it did not enable me to ditch my distress totally, though. But CBT was never going to be enough. I knew that at the outset of asking for help. CBT was a key ingredient like eggs in a good sponge, binding everything else together; the other ingredients being medication, Eye Movement Desensitisation Reprocessing (EMDR), practice, friendship, patience and time.

Love Thyself

Reading the plethora of mindfulness literature out there, we're encouraged to love ourselves. After all, if we don't love ourselves, how can we expect someone else to love us? Besides, we have to live with ourselves 24/7. It makes perfect sense that I have a good, open, honest relationship with myself. That I at least like myself. I've worked at understanding me all my life. No secrets. No illusions. No surprises. I've watched myself grow from a shy, timid, conservative, narrow minded child into a chatty, easy going, learning-to-be liberal, vaguely adventurous woman. At the worst stage of my journey, I hated the me that had PTSD. I was disappointed in her. I thought she was weak, pathetic and selfish. I certainly did not love her. There is more to loving yourself than self-praise, or listing good and bad traits. There is so much more required than being honest with myself: I needed to be kind to me. During CBT I was provided with resources both on line and in print. I delved into these avidly, desperate to acquire the skills to get out of my pit of despair. It became apparent I had to develop self-awareness, self-esteem and self-compassion. I was going to have to learn to do things that would make my body release that magic, kind, caring, good chemicals (oxytocin & opiates); and learn how to stop those bad flight and fright chemicals from flooding my veins (adrenalin & cortisol).

I grew up with a confident and outgoing mother who constantly told me how fabulous, clever and beautiful I was. At the time I was a short, well-covered (aka puppy fat), ginger haired, average child who never got chosen for the netball, squash, hurdle or tennis teams. This low self-esteem did gradually fade as I grew up: I did blossom late, running county and national cross country by seventeen. As mums do, mine told me not to worry about being 'Botticellian' or 'cuddly' as she put it; at least I had reserves if there was another war or famine. My mum told me I had my brains to fall back on and one day I'd become a swan. I took that to mean I was a nerdy, ugly duckling but over time I came to see what she meant. The red hair proved to be an asset in the end, keeping me looking younger as I got older (even though past fifty I cheat nature with a bottle of hair dye); the white skin that had to be religiously kept out of the sun, meant I avoided sun damaged wrinkles, and the tendency to a Botticellian body mass seemed more of a perception than reality in the end once the puppy fat disappeared. I'm proud to be me; I've made the most of my life. I often joked with my husband, that he 'done good' by marrying me, over fifty, fit, still with my own teeth, hair and tits. I'm witty, faithful, loyal and energetic and I earn good money; I can cook, sew, and knit. What more can a husband want?

Self-esteem, as per the guidance on the resources—I went through the process of looking at myself and listing how much I liked about me. Weird thing to do and even more weird to share here, but here goes…… There is a lot to love about me. I joke, but seriously, I am:

Fit (I don't look like the back of a bus)—as the kids say
Smart—physically and mentally
Proud to be ginger—it's kept me looking young
Proud to be Welsh—I make friends easily
A good mum—my kids still talk to me
A decent cook—people look forward to eating my grub
Good with a needle—I designed and made my wedding dress and shortened no end of sleeves and trousers
Quick—I don't waste time
Eloquent—I tend not to bore
Financially stable—I have been able to support my family
Caring—I tend to keep my friends
Honest—I have told a few white lies
Blunt—at least people know what I am thinking most of the time
Stubborn—makes for lively discussions

A bit much sometimes—even for me

A nag—everyone needs a nag and I am happy with that role

Not as patient as I should be—I am working on patience

Irritatingly positive—realists and pessimists give me a wide berth

I wake up happy—I am a good breakfast companion

I push too hard when I think I'm right—someone has to fight incompetence and deceit

I judge too quickly—in my defence I am happy to apologise when proved wrong or insensitive

I talk too much—it's in my genes

I was a fair boss—many of my colleagues are now my friends

I've achieved a lot—and done it my way

I'm not perfect.

Not much irritates me but on my list of things that do:

- Plastic bags
- Ladders in tights
- Long toe nails on men
- Roots showing on dyed hair
- Flies on food

- Dog poo on paths
- People who park on double yellow lines
- Moaners
- Liars
- Clock watchers
- Litter

There are things I get ***really worked*** up about, including:

- Discrimination
- Child abuse
- Sex trafficking
- Rape
- Ignorance

I'm not as arrogant as it may appear; nobody's perfect, I have my weak spots but I've learnt to accept them and this has certainly helped me with my mental well-being. I know I'm hard work to live with; I've had to live with myself for a lifetime. I'm not sure I'd marry me. But truly, I'm proud to be me. I love and have the love of my two children. I loved my mum and had her unconditional love for 57 years. I loved and lost the love for my husband and that's sad, but at least I knew that kind of love.

My therapist asked me to watch some TED Talks on anxiety given by Olivia Remes and I found some gems in her advice, introducing me to the concept of thinking of breakdown as more of a breakthrough. I found this one idea a great way to start self-compassion:

I'm not losing the plot
I'm not sinking into the black hole
I'm not disappearing
I'm taking the time to get help and get better
I'm recognising I have a problem (PTSD) that
    needs fixing and I need help to do it
I cannot keep doing what I'm doing—I need
    to try something new
I need to think differently about myself
Myself—not others—me—me

I need to help me, in the same way I help others, in that OTT way I solve other peoples' problems. I need to focus on me. I am the route to getting back to me. I am strong. I can and I will get better. I have to be patient. There is no short cut.

I'm having a breakthrough

Medication

It is October 2019; I'd been off work for nearly two months and thought it was time to try returning to work. I knew deep down I was still unwell and many friends thought I was not strong enough to go back into a corporate life with all its pressures and responsibilities. But I was Me and I knew better. I couldn't stay hidden away forever. I could go back slowly, part time to Christmas and gradually build up to full time in the New Year (2020). I'd started the CBT and felt things could only get better. But as the date to return to work loomed it hit me; I was still deep in my hole. I was terrified; I still couldn't cope or function. I dreaded the phone ringing, the doorbell buzzing, opening the mail, and driving the car. Up to this point I'd ruled out taking medication. I'd resisted even discussing it. Friends and colleagues gently broached the subject in the initial weeks I was off sick; I would rudely ignore them. I thought taking medication would mean I was:

Giving up
Weak
Dependant

Pathetic
Defeatist

I was at an all-time low; I was extremely tired; tired physically of being down. I didn't know if I could keep going; I was scared I was going backwards not forward. My adrenalin clouds were strong at this juncture of my journey. I was drowning in the fear. I was no longer on the edge of the back hole, I was slipping, sinking, slowly to the bottom. It was not a nice feeling, things felt darker, so very black.

I felt hopeless,
spent,
empty,
so, so empty.

I went to see my GP at the end of October and he questioned my ability to go back to work. I wanted to try, had to try. I bloody had to try. I had to prove to myself I was not disabled by PTSD. I was a bit of a mess and my GP pressed me to reconsider going back to the office. I thought work would allow me to focus on something other than my mental health. I convinced myself the slow return would help. I am not sure I convinced my GP one little bit. During the consultation I'd been crying and pleading and thus it was no surprise that eventually the discussion came around to medication. I resisted vehemently at first, I felt shame at needing drugs. My GP made it clear he had my best interests at heart and at the end of the day he was the doctor. He did not think I could, and should, suffer much more. I agreed to take medication. It is important to understand why I agreed, as this was such a turnaround for me. I agreed to try medication because:

- When I decided to reach out for help, I told myself I'd listen to the professionals
- I could not do things alone anymore—my coping strategies were not enough
- I wanted to be normal, and feel normal consistently
- I wanted to go back to work soon, I needed to concentrate
- I wanted to feel happy and not scared
- I wanted to stop crying
- I had no energy left to keep trying
- I was empty
- I trust my GP
- I didn't trust myself—my self-help/ get out of trouble radar was not working properly

- I wanted someone other than me to make the decisions
- I wanted someone to take the control
- I understood medication may be the catalyst I needed to get back in control
- I wanted my children to see I was getting back on track
- It was time to try something different
- I needed help—urgently

I didn't rush to the chemist to get the medication. First, I spoke with my therapist to solicit her thoughts and she agreed medication in parallel with the program she had lined up for me was sensible. She reassured me that in the UK it's recommended by National Institute for Health and Care Excellence (NICE), and the Royal College of Psychiatrist suggest PTSD should be managed with, CBT, EMDR and medication if clinical signs warrant. I had more than enough clinical signs and symptoms as assessed on the PTSD scale. The medication I'd been prescribed was a selective serotonin reuptake inhibitor (SSRI), commonly used for depression and panic attacks. My GP explained it would take some time, probably months before I saw any noticeable difference to my PTSD. I took my first tablet before bed and it was not long, certainly within the hour, before I felt aware something was happening. At first it felt like I was drowsier, drifting off into sleep, but then I felt like my body perimeter was loosening and my edges were fuzzy and I was drifting away from myself. Not quite out of body but certainly like there were two parts to me. It was a weird feeling. As the night went on, I don't think the medication made much difference to my sleep; I do have trouble going and staying asleep and this night was no different. But when I woke, I was noticeably thirsty. I remained thirsty all the following day. I also felt unbelievably lethargic and exhausted. I fainted when I reached down into my kitchen cupboard. I felt weak; I spent most of the day on the sofa, drifting in and out of sleep. I'd never felt so unconnected. On the second night the same thing happened with me feeling I had fuzzy edges and during the night I was aware my arms and legs were twitching, ever so slightly but it was an odd feeling. Spasm in my arms in particular, like I was trying to flick a fly away. It was like an internal buzz in my muscles. For the first ten days I had a noticeable thirst and night time twitching. The twitches were in the muscles across my neck face and limbs. By the end of two weeks' medication the spasm became much lighter and by six months they were sporadic and mainly at night (after taking a tablet). The thirst lasted about a month; the overwhelming tiredness and lethargy lasted about a week. However, the fainting and feeling faint persisted for weeks and became a little bit of a problem. The feeling faint happened on the way back up from bending or sitting down: when going in cupboards, reaching low supermarket shelves and getting out of some yoga positions. I spoke to a friend's husband who was a clinician and learnt that postural hypotension or orthostatic hypotension was not uncommon when taking SSRIs. I have naturally low blood pressure and was sure this predisposed to me to this, along with the thirst issue and possibly needing to drink even more to keep fully hydrated. The orthostatic hypotension persisted for months but become less of a problem as I learnt how to minimise the drop in blood pressure on standing up by drinking more and moving more slowly and carefully.

The immediate effects of the medication on my PTSD were noticeable within the first month, and certainly by six weeks, which coincided with Christmas. I felt the edge of my anger, self-loathing and anxiety pulled in. I felt less exposed to the extremes of many of my negative emotions. I'd come down a gear with the panic and hyper vigilance. The feelings of fear and dread however persisted for many months at significantly disabling levels. By eight months of taking the medication I felt more harmonious with myself; I was able to accept my negative emotions much more readily; I was slowly building up my confidence and inner strength. I was not back to full strength but my mojo was coming back. Medication gave me space to manage the distressing emotions, and peel away the anxiety that had become my second skin. The daily little white tablet calmed the choppy waters of my PTSD. I had room to stop and take stock. Stop and take stock. Stop and breathe. Stop and relax. Stop and wait. Stop and accept. Stop and remember all the skills I had to hand to blow away the panic, anger and self-doubt.

I get days when I think I am ready to come off the medication and then a very bad day comes along and I realise I'm not there yet. Sometimes I wonder if I would be in a different place if the Covid pandemic had not happened when it did. I'd aimed, hoped, planned and seriously thought I could be off medication within a year of starting it. I am no longer setting myself a target date for that. I am working to get strong and once that point is reached, I can consider the role of medication in my life. I aim to be totally PTSD free one day. Medication has been my buoyancy aid while I learn to swim. I'd have drowned without it. I accepted and needed medication when I was in a crisis and now as I move nearer to the shore of safety, I won't need the life jacket.

EMDR

Once the CBT was finished I felt a little better, but only a little. I felt like a room that had once been full of pain, hurt and agony. I felt as if the CBT had opened the locked doors of the room and given it a jolly good spring clean. I felt space in this room. I could move in the space; I was not hemmed in by the distress. I felt less crowded. But I felt we had not finished in there yet. I could see stubborn corners that had not been fully cleaned out with the CBT. The negative dirt was ingrained into the crevices of my mind and these stubborn stains were going to need more than the CBT broom to get them dealt with for good. I wanted no contaminating thoughts coming back at a later date. I saw EMDR as specialist mind deep cleaning: it was going to be the tool to give me a fresh perspective, sanitising my room, making it safe for me to be there.

I knew EMDR was recommended by NICE in the UK for helping people with non-combat related PTSD. The NICE clinical guidelines are developed by specialists to help the wider medical community, including General Practice, diagnose and manage many health conditions. Although the guidelines have a remit for England specifically, they are considered and referred to within the rest of the UK and more globally. At the time of my writing over 1600 NICE guidance topics were available, from cancer to hypertension, diabetes to asthma and tinnitus to depression. I committed to taking some EMDR sessions because there was clinical evidence it helps people with PTSD. And it did help me.

EMDR is a therapy technique for dealing with distressing or traumatic memories. The theory behind EMDR is that many psychological difficulties are the result of distressing life experiences which have not been stored properly in our memory and these memories are considered to be unprocessed. EMDR helps process the traumatic memories. It's as if the traumatic memories are stored in a raw unprocessed form and thus, they are easily triggered, making them replay as flashbacks and nightmares, causing immediate distress and potentially longer-term harm. EMDR therapy involves attention to three time periods: the past, present, and future. Focus is given to past disturbing memories and related events, and also to current situations that cause distress. The purpose of the treatment is for the person with PTSD to develop the skills and attitudes needed for positive future actions. There are alternative of ways of doing EMDR, always paying attention to bilateral stimulation. Sounds complicated but it's not. While you (as the patient) recall any emotionally disturbing memories, you have to focus simultaneously on an external stimulus provided by the therapist. Therapist directed lateral eye movements are the most commonly used external stimulus.

Initially we tried this common method of me following with my eyes (not head) my therapist finger as she moved it from left to right in my line of vision. I felt sick and dizzy with this method and it was irritating as I was never sure if I wanted my varifocal glasses on or off during the processing. What actually worked for me was sitting square to my therapist, with my eyes closed, whilst my therapist tapped alternatively and rhythmically on my left and right knees. During the tapping my hands relaxed on my thighs and breathing deeply and calmly, I'd recall the memory and focus on what I felt. It is not as easy as it sounds, it did take me a few times to get in the groove of EMDR: I had to practice shutting out random thoughts, practice tracing the memory. Truly trace the trauma in as much detail as I could muster, visually, aurally and olfactorily.

EMDR is a stepwise approach and step one is the preparation phase. The first thing I had to do was identify a troubling memory and the most horrific moment and image of that memory. This was hard for me; I had so many horrific memories, I didn't know which one to recall. I decided to focus on the near fatal asthma attack of December 2005. The memory was the scream of my little boy having a heart attack, me pushing the emergency button on the back wall of his ward bed, a crash team arriving out of nowhere, a medic doing CPR, doctors and nurses in action, babies sleeping undisturbed on the children's ward despite the noise of the emergency and me standing there heavy, frozen and bloody scared, before I passed out.

The next part of the preparation phase involved me having to identify a negative belief about the worst moment. For me it was that I could not save my child. I then had to identify emotions and bodily feeling linked to that moment. This required no conscious thought; just talking about it made me feel sick, heavy, terrified, mouth dry, stomach dropped to my toes, legs shaking, heart racing, and that heavy down pull before passing out. During preparation I also had to pull up a good memory to have a safe place to go to if needed. I thought of the spectacular view I had from my bedroom window as a teenager of a Norman castle, nestled on a hill above the Tywi estuary. I had to describe this memory in detail and recall the good feelings this safe memory evoked. Even today I metaphorically revisit this safe place, bringing to mind the magical landscape, the flat sands framing the climb to the battlements, and the salty smell of the sea mixing with the sweet woody wafts of fern.

Anyway, back to 2020 and getting ready for EMDR. In addition to the safe place, I needed to have to hand a bank of people to be my companions. People I could call on, as it were, when I was struggling, a sort of 'phone a friend'. My therapist asked me to identify three figures, real or imagined, past or present that fulfilled the roles of my protector, my nurturer and my advisor. I chose my GP to fulfil the latter role and my daughter for my protector and nurturer. These were two people I knew I could trust and I could readily imagine what their input would look, sound and feel like, as in a way they both had been fulfilling the roles for a while. I fell back on these companions many times during the EMDR, so much so that I often felt as if they were in the room. It made me feel less alone, less ashamed to be in need of help, less hurt.

Step two of EMDR is called the processing phase and here I was asked to think about the image and belief, while at the same time as paying attention to the tapping on my knees. I was instructed to allow my mind to go with whatever came up and just notice what happened. The process was repeated until I was able to recall the memory with little distress. This took a lot out of me. At first my mind wandered and even when I was in the zone I got upset and cried and had to jump to my safe place, my view of the castle over the Tywi estuary. I struggled sometimes keeping to the one memory as my thoughts flitted to the other near-death events; my brain became overloaded with these mixed memories and I wrestled with controlling them; I had to keep going with the flow, following the thread and this was mentally and physically taxing.

I saw EMDR as the vehicle to re-park my bad memories. By the time we were coming to the end of the course, I knew it was a powerful means of routing out my hidden thoughts, fears, aspirations, doubts and recollections. During the sessions I voiced things I'd never had on my conscious radar. I surprised myself with the thoughts that popped out of my mind and mouth. Sometimes the thought flows were disturbing and upsetting and other times they were refreshing and enlightening. Crying was a big part of the sessions but the tears were cleansing. I felt all the better for sobbing. The sessions were physically demanding: my heart pounding, my palms sweating, my mouth drying up, and that sinking feeling in your belly when staring disaster in the face and the shit is hitting the fan. The memories of the asthma attacks felt real; cruelly real during EMDR.

During EMDR sessions the therapist monitors your ability to tolerate the distressing memory, using a 1 to 10 scale. Over the weeks of therapy, we inched from 10 (bloody awfully distressing) to 2/3 (acceptable, not too bad). I can live with that: if I choose to think about my memories, I know they will remain upsetting, but not distressing, and that is the important difference. Having a choice to think about the bad stuff rather than it being an unwanted, uninvited guest is a success; no intrusion is a great cure.

EMDR sessions made me think in pictures. I had extremely strong, vivid and real images during the sessions. My fear was represented by a cloak; it was heavy and black and enveloped me in the dark times. The cloak was dense and seemed to follow me, only ever inches from my back and shoulders. I felt its presence like an oppressive heat you feel, but cannot touch or see. As I moved through the EMDR sessions the cloak distanced itself from me and I felt lighter; eventually towards the end of the twelve sessions I was turning around to face the cloak. It seemed less dark when I looked at it directly. I was eventually able to hang the cloak up on its own peg and leave it there.

The EMDR sessions left me unbelievably exhausted; I felt like I'd been in a tumble drier after each session.

EMDR involves a lot of recalling and reliving the traumatic event (or tracing the trauma as I came to explain it to others) and so for me there was a lot of crying. Cathartic but draining crying. I often cried all the way home in the car after these sessions. Once I met my daughter in a café after a session and we hid in the corner behind the thankfully humongous cheese plant while I sobbed my heart out. Another customer kindly and quietly slid a packet of tissues to me between the foliage and surreptitiously paid for us to have another coffee I learnt quickly not to wear make up to my EMDR sessions and to scheduled nothing for the rest of the day. In the early sessions, (the first six) I was wiped out for the rest of the week, I was emotionally drained. In total I had twelve sessions over a three-month period. Throughout the course of the EMDR my therapist monitored my progress, so we could iron out any stubborn negative beliefs and we regularly discussed how I was benefitting from the therapy.

At best PTSD is a predicament and at its worst, a prison. EMDR enabled me to face the fear and feel it. Really feel it. Then and only then could I let it go. After reliving and describing the trauma it was the release of the fear that was ultimately curative. Not remembering and discussing the traumas is what had kept me stuck. Forgetting about the shit and just moving on had kept me trapped for over a decade. I stopped EMDR at a natural juncture in late February of 2020; in part I wanted a rest from therapy so I could consolidate everything, and besides I'd some significant travel plans lined up. I had found the guts to agree to go to Granada (Spain) in April with friends and booked a holiday in Grenada (Caribbean) for my children and me for late May.

On completing the EMDR I felt fragile. I know I had come far with getting to grips with the PTSD, but I was in no way back to full strength. I was still evolving. It was as if I'd been taken apart, limb by limb and put back together and the glue was not quite set. I was in the right shape to face the future, but I was wobbly. I still had my stabilisers on (medication) and until the glue set, I was not to be put under too much pressure. EMDR helped with eliminating the flashbacks and intrusive thoughts; it helped lessen the frequency and horror of my nightmares. This was a great step forward, and gave me the courage and determination to keep going. I believed, wanted and knew that one day I would be free of PTSD and that I would reappear in all my glory. I was not totally cured but I was well on the way to being back to me; back to feeling safe, secure and brave. I was near back to coping with life, being independent, and that unbearable Me. Little did I know, Covid-19 was coming.

My Worst Nightmare

I'd been fully off work with PTSD for September and October of 2019; during November and December I tried a phased return to work starting with two days and building up to three by the Christmas break. With hindsight returning to work so soon was a really bad idea, but at least I'd tried and that made me feel good. However, returning to work in the New Year of 2020 I realised I was fragile, vulnerable, and still bloody scared. By February I was unable to carry on working and signed off sick once more.

Now it's fair to say we'd not had a restful Christmas. During the 2019 Christmas break my daughter had been very sick. The run up to her illness had been stressful for us all. Whilst my children had been away to see their father, my daughter had started to get a horrific headache, followed by vomiting and a temperature. Most illnesses tend to trigger my daughter's epilepsy and thus they decided to set off for home earlier than planned. The five-hour journey home was hell: my son, a newly qualified driver, was understandably anxious about his sister, who was becoming delirious and vomiting profusely. They had a bucket in the car, but there were times they had to stop quickly for her to throw up. My son had a black box fitted to his car as part of the insurance and later he noticed his score had gone from 93% (good driving) to 51% (poor driving). Stopping on dual carriage ways and the M4 hard shoulders was not good driving and the Black Box knew it. My son was so worried about his sister's condition at one point that he thought of dialling 999 from a service station. When I took a call from my son as they were half way home, I could hear the anxiety and fear in his voice. I felt sick and started to shake as I heard how ill my daughter was getting. None of us felt comfortable with the situation but the thought of her being whisked to a hospital by an ambulance nowhere near home was a concern; I told him to drive slowly and carefully and just focus on the road.

During the 3 hours wait till they arrived home, my PTSD reared its ugly head. The dark cloak of fear crowded my thoughts and all I could think was that both my children would die on the motorway. I had vivid thoughts of a terrible fatal crash. When they eventually arrived home, I burst into tears. Tears of joy and relief. They were alive and home. Home and safe. Most of the next day, Christmas Eve, was spent in our GP surgery while my daughter was examined and closely monitored, but by Boxing Day she had deteriorated so badly she was admitted to hospital. My daughter was very sick and despite a battery of clinical tests it was agreed she had one of the nasty viruses that were going around. It was a nasty virus indeed; it took four long weeks for her to recover and regain her strength. Luckily, my son and I didn't catch this bugger of a germ, and we remained well throughout.

The death of my children has been a big part of my nightmares with PTSD. And it was thus no surprise that the thoughts of both my children dying in a car accident continued over the first few weeks of 2020. I had to hold onto all the lessons I'd learnt in CBT to be able to function. I recognised the fear but it was cripplingly overwhelming and some days I struggled to do anything. At the time I was going through the last few sessions of EMDR and thus had the chance to deal with these nightmares in my sessions. I started to feel better; certainly, less scared my children would die. I felt I was getting a grip on the PTSD. My children were not dead. I knew that. I felt scared but I knew my children were alive. Fifteen love to me.

During the Christmas and New Year period we were mildly aware of the situation developing in China with Coronavirus; by mid-January the WHO had confirmed one death and 41 cases related to the new respiratory virus. By February 2020 the news of the British family of five in the French Alps was hitting the headlines and I was mildly concerned about the threat of a pandemic in the UK. As details about the virus and its spread started being a feature of the daily news, I begin to unravel. My life was walking before me across the very, very, thin ice of a deep, dark lake. By March the Covid threat was not confined to cruise ship holiday makers or Wuhan residents. It was here in the UK. Monday March 2nd—40 Covid cases in the UK—Wednesday 4th March 85 cases and by 10th March 373 cases and six dead.

Dead.
Dead.
Dead.

It was as if all the good work, effort, CBT, mindfulness, EMDR, patience, self-compassion and progress had been dashed; washed away with the 6 O'clock news. This was real. Very real. There was a virus creeping around the UK with the potential to kill my children. Covid-19 was a genuine threat to both my children and one I had to face. If they got Covid-19 neither would fare well: my son with his history of life-threatening asthma and my daughter with epilepsy. I was shit scared my children would die of coronavirus. Covid-19 was my worst nightmare and it was real, it was here. My actual nightmares got worse, both in frequency and distress; they became a mix of real events and potential fears. My head was mixing up the past and making up a future. I tried to hide the anguish of these nightmares but I was all too often screaming in my sleep and waking the house up again.

I was certainly not overdramatising the potential of Covid to kill my kids. I really wasn't. My sons' triggers for his life-threatening asthma attacks were quite specific. Long standing cold or chest infection, usually viral, followed by dramatic changes in weather conditions or close exposure to cats (as in sleepovers at cat-owning friends). My daughter has little resistance to any type of infections, having been hospitalised Boxing Day of 2019 for a viral infection and 2016 for Periorbital Cellulitis (an eye infection which she has had three times to date). Both of them were (and still are) high risk of getting a bad reaction to a Covid-19 infection. My anxiety was through the roof. I could not stop myself from watching the news bulletins. I thought if I had enough knowledge and information, I could stop any harm coming our way; I could micro-manage our way through this safely. But the constant sight of ITU beds in countries all over the world, from China and Italy to the UK was fuelling my PTSD. I could smell the scenes on the news. I felt as if I was there. I heard the bleep of the monitors and the hiss of the nebulisers above the news correspondents. I was there, I was really there. I was inside the TV, shaking and scared. I was back in ITU all over again.

Back Pocket

Having tried and tested ways to help deal with problems is something I encouraged my kids and staff to acquire. It's good to have toolkit full of useful instruments to mend something; it's great to have a back pocket full of essential reserves to hand. I considered my to-do and not-to lists part of my toolkit. Over time I added some new skills to my back pocket; things I could pull out quickly to help me cope when I was in a bad place When I first struggled with PTSD, I found it helped to write things down. I wrote my story of those difficult times as the awful things happened. I was a prolific scribbler. I would sit at the PC for hours at a time and rattle the events out. Writing it down helped me get the pain out. It was cathartic cleansing at the time. Putting it on the page was all I could do though. Even today, over ten years on I can't look back at what I wrote; it hurts to read my own story. But over a decade later, I initially struggled to write anything down. I could not focus or sit at the PC. It was as if there was a block in my brain. I could not think. It hurt too much to see how terrible I felt in words, in print. It seemed to make things unavoidably real if I wrote it down. I could not lie to the page; I could not put on a brave face for it. More to the point, where would I start; there was so much in my head. I had so many feelings and thoughts, so much going on in my life. Incongruously I was able to talk. I'd no problem talking to those close to me. I could go from brain to mouth, describing how disabling things were, quite openly. In time I grew bored of my own voice. I grew bored of my own story. I wanted to get the pain out by talking about it, getting it out, getting it out; but I felt like a stuck record. I was bored of being sick, of being off work, keeping it under control. I was tired of all the control, all the effort to stay reasonable and functioning.

Bored
Stuck
Bored
Stuck
Bored
Stuck
Repeat

I wanted to hide. I wanted to stop. I wanted the pain and fear to end. I wanted to run away. My head told me there was nowhere to run to, hiding was not the answer. I have to move forward and face the problem. Hiding will just make me more scared, hiding will feed the fear. I have to get better, get help, and recognise the cause of this problem; know the enemy in my head.

During EMDR I had to recall the trauma and follow the thread of thoughts and feelings. I found this therapy surprising powerful and the images it provoked were almost tangible. Off the back of this approach, I decided to spend time recalling the good times of my life. I would think of something good and pull out the sights sounds and smells. I would feel the light; feel the joy of the happy times in my life. As before, I used photograph albums to help. This simple exercise was uplifting. Sometimes I'd cry and other times I'd be in stiches, laughing. During the exercise I made sure to concentrate on how I felt. More often than not I felt positive feelings; joy, excitement, anticipation, enthusiastic, delight, energetic, happiness, pride, fulfilment and contentment. I recalled my wedding day. I'd made my own dress in gold satin; I looked a million dollars. I'd bought the fabric in a top department store in London for a bargain price in 1985. The fabric had a flaw at one-meter intervals and this made it nigh on impossible for most people to use. But as I'm short I could cut the pattern within the flaw; I negotiated to have the 10-meter roll for £60 instead of £60 per meter. It was easy enough to negotiate the price, it was quite another to negotiate carrying it home on the London Underground and British Rail. We did a very much home-made wedding, making all the attendants' outfits, the wedding cake and photograph album; the day was wonderful. The sun shone all day despite it being late spring in Wales. Recalling my wedding day, I felt nostalgic, happy and proud.

On my first child, I was walking around the hospital to keep upright when my waters broke. I was wandering in the geriatric section of the hospital, quite away from maternity and this caused quite a commotion; one of patients gave up his wheelchair so my husband could zoom me back to maternity; leaving the cleaning staff dealing with the flood I'd created. Recalling the birth of my children I felt, fulfilled, content and invincible, and lucky. I spent hours leafing through the photograph albums of the kids as babies. Like most parents we took hundreds of photos of our firstborn; baby in bath, baby eating breakfast, baby with granny, baby with daddy, baby in the pram, baby smiling, baby sleeping. Photos of baby 1 at one to fifty-two weeks. By the time our second was born we were tired and busy and the photos reflected that; baby after birth, baby being dragged about by sister and baby age three, six months and a year at best.

I recalled the wonderful family holidays we'd had in Wales, France, Menorca and the Azores. I saw the children splashing about in the sea, two little people jumping and surfing over the waves. I reminisced about all the castles we'd explored, our picnics on the beach rain or shine. I smelt the salty air. I tasted the sand in the cheese and pickle sandwiches. I remembered the time the kids had swum in the mid-Atlantic with dolphins and whales whilst on holiday in the Azores (you wouldn't be allowed to do this anymore). Thinking of these times I felt joyful and adventurous. I felt good. I felt alive. I found this exercise helped me; I still spend time going down happy memory lane and feeling it.

During my working life I had to negotiate on an almost daily basis. I truly enjoyed negotiation because it meant getting to know a party or person in some detail. It involved communication and the building and maintaining of relationships. If I managed to secure a successful settlement then there was a trust in place that set me up for future co-operation. I'd listen very carefully during a negotiation; I'd try to understand what the other party wanted and why; I tried to clarify what their drivers and pressures were. I'd come at the negotiation with the aim of finding a win: win solution, where both parties felt we'd agreed a good deal. When things went well, we all felt good, because we'd all won. Negotiation takes time and patience; it requires some element of emotional control. Emotion in negotiation has a valid role and I learnt how to channel mine effectively. People tend to listen when you tell them how you feel (as long as you don't overdo it and the response is valid); No-one can say you did not feel that way, even if they would have felt differently.

I negotiated with my fear, that black cloak that followed me around, and in times of distress it pressed heavily on my back and shoulders, forcing me down and under. I turned and looked at the fear. Looked directly at it, no matter how scared I was, and acknowledged it was there. I decided if I listened to the fear, rather than ignoring it, it would stop shouting at me. I'd give the fear air time, try to understand what it wanted and why. I tried to think of it as a person who had their own pressures. I had to find a win: win solution or the fear had the potential to overcome and destroy me. So, I was patient, and on some days let the fear have dominance, but I'd make it clear it was just for a day, hour or spell, whatever I had strength to withstand. Then it would be time for the fear to be quiet and listen to me. I even talked to the fear. 'I know why you're shouting and that is fine for now, but we can't keep doing this, it's not good for either of us. I want to find a solution. I want to help you. I want to feel strong again and when you shout at me, I feel weak.' I was not in any way schizophrenic but the process helped me give space to deal with the fear. Over time and with the EMDR making a positive difference I was able to manage the fear and dread.

For most of my life I believed I didn't do anxiety and thus reasoned I didn't have the skills and experience to deal with it. I truly thought I was at a disadvantage, that my positive 'I can cope' nature was now a handicap as I'd not learnt to cope with anxiety. But on account of the self-compassion training, I came to rethink this. I came to understand I did have the skills to deal with anxiety: I'd been doing so most of my life. PTSD apart, I am a smiling, mostly coping and the majority of time happy person, happy and glad to be alive.

Research suggests that people who feel, or are in control of their life, people who forgive themselves (don't beat themselves up for no reason) and people who are needed and feel needed (people who have a purpose), deal with anxiety well. I hope I'm not delusional but I believe I've got these resources. I may well take the control thing too far, I may well not forgive myself all the time, but in the main I don't do unnecessary guilt. I look at a problem or situation and think 'what can I do to make it better?' Better, not perfect. What can I do practically? This means I tend to take action and not allow myself to feel but I do consider what emotions may be involved, especially the emotions of those involved, I just don't let them dictate or dominate my next step. During my recovery I began to pick this thinking apart to understand how to manage my emotional side, especially negative emotions. If the research is true, re coping resources, then I have been dealing with anxiety all my life and until recently I'd been doing okay. It's just that at the moment I'm not able to benefit from those resources. Something has got stuck, something is blocking my normal ability to cope with anxiety and fear. I'm stuck in flight-fright-freeze mode. I have PTSD. I have to take care of myself for a while.

When you have a chronic condition that tends to flare up, whether that be migraine or eczema, asthma or IBS, hay fever or epilepsy, you get to know what triggers the condition off. You do this so you can avoid or limit the headaches, the itching, the wheezing, the bloating, the blocked nose and even the fits. PTSD is no different and my new mental health hygiene titbits involved:

- Knowing my triggers
- Spotting my behaviour signs
- Telling others what to look out for
- Giving specific people authority to challenge me if they see the signs

I spoke to those around me about the signs and gave them authority to step in. Many times I was not aware I was slipping into a worry vortex, one of the first signs being my cleaning of floors and muddled thinking which led to me being quiet. A quiet Me is a Me in trouble. A Me avidly cleaning is a Me in distress. Having people point out my behaviour was an easy way to monitor my recovery. No need to fill in a mental health questionnaire, or answer tricky questions or recall how I felt last week or month: it was instant, objective and factual. I could not argue with, deflect or escape my behaviour. Pointing out stopped me spiralling down further. I can live with silence but not strain. I can live with dirt but not distress.

Courage & Hope

In the early days of my journey with PTSD I didn't understand the relationship between courage and hope. I considered them very different emotions, each end of a spectrum; I didn't have much time for hope. I'd never felt comfortable considering it as a positive or constructive verb (or emotion). As a doing word there never seemed to me much doing involved in it. Wishing or wanting never got me anywhere. I could not relate to Dostoevsky's thought that 'To live without hope is to cease to live.' I'd tell myself 'You don't need hope; you need courage in the face of danger. You have to dig deep when you're scared, in pain or grief. You need more than hope when you are alone in a nightmare. No point hoping, do something.' I was more aligned to the thinking of Disraeli, 'Action may not always bring happiness; but there is no happiness without action.' I'm not dissing hope. I'm being honest about how I felt for a very long time. If you're reading this book it's likely you hope to find some help, useful advice or something to relate to. I would not dream of dashing anyone's hope. Keep reading. You do have to do something to get stronger, to get better. Facing the issues, admitting the pain, accepting the help and even resting are all active and courageous things to do. I learnt that.

When my youngest was growing up, we watched the film *The Lord of the Rings: The Two Towers* (2002, directed by Peter Jackson) over and over again. The journeys of Frodo Baggins and Samwise Gamgee were arduous, darkness and evil on every side, with seen and unseen monsters. The courageous words (adaptation in the film from Tolkien's book) of Samwise to Frodo as they are on the way to the Battle of Osgiliath ring in my ears, 'I know. It's all wrong. By rights we shouldn't even be here. But we are. It's like in the great stories, Mr. Frodo. The ones that really mattered. Full of darkness and danger they were. And sometimes you didn't want to know the end. Because how could the end be happy? How could the world go back to the way it was when so much bad had happened? But in the end, it's only a passing thing, this shadow. Even darkness must pass. A new day will come. And when the sun shines it will shine out the clearer. Those were the stories that stayed with you. That meant something, even if you were too small to understand why. But I think, Mr. Frodo, I do understand. I know now. Folk in those stories had lots of chances of turning back, only they didn't. They kept going, because they were holding on to something.' Wikipedia defines courage as 'the choice and willingness to confront agony, pain, danger, uncertainty, or intimidation'. Being courageous when you have PTSD is all about holding on; I choose not to turn back, just like Sam and Frodo. PTSD felt like a mountain I had to climb; I was daunted by the peak, the scale of the problem. I knew there'd be sharp edges of rock, steep inclines, and times I'd not be able to see the summit. I had to keep climbing; I had to have courage. There were times I thought my stamina would run out. At each juncture of understanding on the way up this mountain I realised there was much I didn't know or understand. I'd not been this way before. I was relying on my guides (therapist, GP and close friends and family) to get me successfully to the top. Over quoted, but I get why Plato thought 'Courage is a kind of salvation. Courage is knowing what not to fear.' and Napoleon said 'Courage isn't having the strength to go on—it's going on when you don't have strength.'

I had to be careful and patient, not traits that come naturally to me. I had to pace myself as there was no point rushing to the top of my mountain unless I had the stamina, skill, strength and ability to climb back down. Recovery was the way up the mountain and resilience was the way down. I think of understanding as mainly a sequential process, there is some order to our acquiring knowledge; it's how we tend to be taught. We first learn our numbers, then we learn to count one to ten, one to hundred, and once we have mastered that we move on to addition, multiplication and division and then on to more complex maths. It's a linear process, building on prior knowledge, having a foundation of understanding and making our learning efficient:

No wasting time
Making fewer mistakes
Limited errors
Structure
Certainty

I wanted to be ultra-efficient in dealing with my PTSD. However, I found understanding my mind and feelings un-sequential. Knowledge and understanding did not seem to run in parallel. Just because I knew something did not mean I understood it or even more to the point, that I felt it. There was no certainty about my mind. Relaxation is a good example. I know what relaxation is; why we need to relax, what happens when you relax, different ways to relax etc...... But most of the time I didn't feel truly relaxed. I feigned it sometimes in the hope the real thing would appear out of pity. I remember in my NCT (National Child Birth Trust) classes when asked to relax, hissing to my friend, 'whose got time to relax, we're all about to have a baby and then go back to work? Relax, that's not on my to-do list.' I was wrong, relax should be on all to-do lists, even mine.

There was no set process for building a foundation that would ensure I understood all my feelings; the healing was going to be individualistic. No two people are the same. I was going to have to be open, flexible and go with the flow. During my recovery I was enlightened in quite random ways and it felt catalytic. One piece of new insight seemed to connect many more dots and spark off new thoughts and good feelings. I didn't have to understand or know to feel. I just had to have the courage to feel.

Feel happy or sad
Feel safe or scared
Feel better or worse
Feel frustrated or empowered
Feel free or trapped
Feel blameless or guilty
Feel confused or lucid
Feel vulnerable or strong
Feel on top of the world or down in the dumps
Feel hopeful
Feel alive

So, what about hope? It was whilst discussing this bucket with my daughter that I eventually understood the relationship between hope and courage. It took a person with more wisdom and less years to remind me to be kind, kind to myself and kind to humanity. My daughter pointed out that this way of thinking was typical me, doing not feeling. I saw action and courage as good; I saw inaction and hope as weak. This was not progress. My daughter sees hope as being able to imagine a future, wanting a future and it is this imagination and wanting that inspires our courage. Where would we be as humans without hope? I am writing this book in the middle of the coronavirus pandemic and as if that is not bad enough, the news is heavy with the deaths of innocent peoples across the world due to racism, famine, war, terrorism, or freak weather. Today as I write, I hope for an end to the Covid pandemic (as we witness a successful vaccination program in the UK), an end to religious and racial intolerance, and an end to corruption and global warming. I get hope with that caveat. It makes sense. Having hope is what makes us human. It dispels darkness. Just feeling hopeful brushes away at the edges of gloom. It helps me picture the better places and plan for a future. Hope inspires and feeds my courage. I get hope now, and that feels good.

"Little do ye know your own blessedness; for to travel hopefully is a better thing than to arrive, and the true success is to labour."

Robert Louis Stevenson quotation,
from *Virginibus Puerisque* (1881)

Tryst & Trust

Tryst—I love this word. Roll it around your tongue. Even its synonyms are evocative words—rendezvous, assignation, encounter and tête-à-tête. I found that making sure I put time in my diary to meet or talk to people helped me stopped slipping back into the black hole. And even when in the bottom of my pit of despair I found it helpful to have people send down a bucket of love and kindness. I would 'walk and talk', 'march and moan,' and I was fortunate to have friends that would 'stride and support' (aka listen). I'd put these appointments in my diary when I felt strong. When I felt fragile and scared, these dates were still there; if I was tempted to cancel them or back out, then my friends would take action to reach into the pit so I was not left to suffer alone, or in silence.

> "A friend is, as it were, a second self."
> Cicero

I was never truly alone during my recovery from PTSD as I had the trust of a small group of friends and that of my two kids. I only actually, physically, had a few months living by myself when I was first off sick in the autumn of 2019. I was, in fact, glad to be alone at that time. I was glad my son had left home for a new job and was happy that my daughter was busy with her job in London. My husband and I had been separated for just over a year. Alone in my home, I could just be me; me with PTSD. I did not have to hide behind a mum, wife or boss mask. Besides I had my friends who were always ready to walk and talk. For a few months this seclusion was fine; it gave me time to think and rest. But as the end of the year approached, I was struggling again: I'd been back at work part time for a few weeks and I was boxing off my anxiety, dread and fear all over again. I was not coping. But I kept my brave face on. In the New Year of 2020 my daughter came back home to live with me. It was to prove beneficial to both of us in many ways, particularly when the Covid pandemic broke. For some of the most difficult times of my recovery, my daughter was by my side. I did not have to face things alone anymore.

I had the:
love,
support,
practical help,
tenderness,

company,
humour,
guidance,
honesty,
direction,
empathy,
kindness,
and care of my daughter.

My daughter's insight and advice stopped me from unravelling, going back to my old ways and habits of dealing with shit. She helped me rewind the threads of my life neatly back up, undoing any knots along the way. She never let me lose sight of who I was, who I am and who I will always be. Me.

We laughed and cried during our months of Covid confinement. My daughter showed me how to relax properly through yoga, use WhatsApp with good manners, access literature through audiobooks, and cook (and eat) vegan meals. I have never, and will never, consider my daughter as my best friend. She is my daughter and I am her mother and that is a wonderfully fulfilling relationship; it lasts a lifetime. It is a relationship built on trust and history; it is precious and to be respected. I can't imagine how arduous and slow my recovery would have been without her. She was my thermometer, letting me know when the PTSD was boiling over.

Trusting someone comes easily to some people. Not to me. I have spoken to many of my women friends whose life has not been a bed of roses, either because of breast cancer, an alcoholic family member, abuse, drug problems with their kids and divorce; and to so many of us trust does not come naturally. I had learnt to cope with life and at no point along that path did anyone show me how to trust. They say trust has to be earned, not learned? Who knows what comes first, learning or earning? But the plus side of having PTSD is that I learnt to trust a few people; people who freely gave me their time, love, honesty, support and friendship. Given with no obligation or judgement. If someone gives, then good manners dictate there has to be someone to receive (with grace and thanks) and so I opened myself up to accepting and trusting. And it felt good. I felt safe. Trust took the edge off my fear. Trust dampened the dread and dispelled the despair. I wish you could order trust off Amazon.

Books That Made It Better

Many of the self-help books I read didn't really tell me how it felt to be depressed: anxious, scared, angry, frustrated, empty, terrified or lonely; and more to the point what it looked like. I couldn't get a clear picture of what these feelings might manifest as in terms of behaviour. My reading reminded me of being pregnant, when people who'd not had children gave me advice, or told me what it felt like, when giving birth or breast feeding; how the hell would they know what it felt like, and thus what the best thing to do, was? Many of the books I read were clean and clinical, written by well qualified psychologist and I don't deny they offered genuinely sensible advice. Advice I did take in the long run, when I was stronger. But I came at these books when I was drowning. I was chest deep in emotional shit, strangled by fear. At the time I was reading the books, I was slipping into deep despair and the advice was of limited value for me. I could not reach it: I had lost my perspective and my ability to think clearly. The advice was great for those whose mental health problem was not yet a crisis, or disabling. I resorted to reading and listening to stories about people: people who'd shown courage. I chomped through a wide selection of memoirs, autobiographies, biographies, diaries, a few novels and some poetry. After each story I came away with a lesson and renewed resolution to keep going, to thrive. I was not alone, suffering is widespread.

I Know Why the Caged Bird Sings
Maya Angelou

I cried when I read this book.

Lesson Learnt: You can turn trauma into triumph by committing thoughts to writing. Writing helps you make sense of the horror that has happened, draw meaning from it, and move forward with more insight and understanding. Don't carry the pain. Do something with it.

When Breath Becomes Air
Paul Kalanithi

Lesson Learnt: Even in the face of death we can still keep living, learning and loving. Death is not the end of our life; we can choose to leave a legacy. We can learn what it means to be human even when our identity is changed by illness.

I am Malala
Malala Yousafzai

Lesson Learnt: Courage cannot be destroyed by domination or intimidation. Words from the pen of a child have the power to crush extremism peacefully. Courage begins at a young age.

One Day in the Life of Ivan Denisovich
Aleksandr Solzhenitsyn

Lesson Learnt: No matter how much shit gets shovelled your way, no matter how much inhumanity you are subjected to, how much injustice comes your way, how long you face oppression, remember this, we were born to be free and we need to protect our freedom. We all have a choice to be humane.

Infidel, Nomad
Ayaan Hirsi Ali

Lessons Learnt: We all have a backstory, family history and cultural influences that shape who we are. If we seek to change our path in life and do so in the face of family and cultural resistance it's a lonely and scary journey to pursue. Having the courage to change countries and cultures to get your freedom is courage personified.

The Tattooist of Auschwitz, & Cilka's Journey
Heather Morris

Lessons Learnt: In the face of tyranny and oppression human beings can become stronger, more resourceful and ingenious than they ever believed themselves possible of. To survive such emotional and physical degradation and starvation without becoming vengeful or consumed by hate is truly inspirational. And because we humans are hard wired to feel, we can still love even when surrounded by cruelty, prejudice, ignorance, indifference and brutality.

Henry's Demons
Patrick and Henry Cockburn

Lesson Learnt: Mental illness is a family matter, in more ways than one. The impact of a mental health diagnosis, in this case schizophrenia, has consequences that you cannot imagine at the start of the journey; it really is a bumpy passage for all involved and it's impossible to be fully prepared. I identified with the need of, and effort by, Henry's parents to understand why Henry had schizophrenia. Some of us think if we understand we will cope better: the difficulty is understanding the places inside someone else's head, and sometimes even your own.

Hillbilly Elegy: A memoir of a family and culture in crisis
J D Vance

Lesson Learnt: Life can deal you a bum hand but some humans have the courage and grace to forgive those that made their life hell. Some people have the power to move on despite a shit legacy and the demons that never leave. I was inspired by the love J D Vance had for those that caused his trauma. The author does not mention PTSD but does refer to terrifying dreams. I was challenged with the questions throughout the book on responsibility, and looking ourselves in the mirror to considering how we personally (and our communities) can make things better.

As I grew stronger and had started my cathartic writing I read two self-help books written by Matt Haig recommended to me by my daughter, and an old book on nerves by Claire Weeks, recommended to me by a friend who has struggled with depression for a significant part of his adult life. Both authors deal very well with fear and anxiety, providing practical tips for coping, and despite the very different language and style of writing, these authors had me nodding in agreement as they painted pictures of being overwhelmed.

Reasons to Stay Alive
Matt Haig

Lessons Learnt: You might be seriously depressed but you can be funny—very funny. Humour helps. People suffering mental health have an amazing capacity to act and thus look normal—we are great deceivers and this has the potential to cost lives.

Notes on a Nervous Planet
Matt Haig

Lesson learnt: How to live in a mad world without ourselves going mad. Working out what about the world makes us feel sad or scared, confused or ill, calm and happy; finding the world we want to live in, and remembering the world exists inside us but the world is not our feelings. We can contradict ourselves and the world. We have the right to be ourselves.

Self Help for Your Nerves
Dr Claire Weeks

Lesson Learnt: Despite this being a rather outdated view on mental health, having been first published in 1962, the insight and descriptions of the physical aspects of fear and anxiety were spot on—mental illness shows up in all parts of your body. It is important to recognise that recovery may not rest only in your own hands, and that most people need help; not to feel ashamed or discouraged if you do need help (page 68). Early training/ upbringing can help or hinder our ability to cope with a 'nervous illness' and although not in reference to PTSD, try not to extinguish unpleasant feelings before they are established, instead face them. The Chinese proverb that ends the book says much to me 'Trouble (aka PTSD) is a tunnel through which we pass and not a brick wall against which we must break our head.' I can get better.

You Learn by Living: Eleven Keys for a More Fulfilling Life
Eleanor Roosevelt

Lesson Learnt: Living is for learning. We should not ignore the experiences life deals us, good or bad. We must use them to shape our thinking and create a better world. Although this book was published in 1960 when views on mental health were very different, Eleanor epitomises a kind, caring, independent, no-nonsense, rational voice. Her views on self-knowledge, self-discipline and the right to be an individual could have been written yesterday. I found her comments on enabling and encouraging children to speak their mind in preparation for adulthood refreshing and modern, #*You have an obligation to be an individual.*

Many people I spoke to about depression specifically encouraged me to read poetry; apparently in the 13th Century the books of the Italian poet, Dante were sold in apothecary shops: literature as medicine. I could not face Dante but my children and friends had lighter suggestions.

Alone
Maya Angelou

Clips from Maya's poems are littered throughout the internet on 'looking for a poignant quote' type sites, but one should really read her poems from a book. This woman was amazing and through her poems you can touch the reality of loss and hardship. But somehow when I read them, especially when I read them aloud, I feel inspired to keep going.

A Psalm of Life
Henry Wadsworth Longfellow

My favourite nursey rhyme is,' 'There was a little girl', written by Henry Wadsworth Longfellow. From his 'A Psalm of Life' Lesson Learnt: life is for living, be ready for what comes my way and remember I have the chance to leave directions to the lost that follow me:

> "Lives of great men all remind us
> We can make our lives sublime,
> And, departing, leave behind us
> Footprints on the sands of time;

Footprints, that perhaps another,
Sailing o'er life's solemn main,
A forlorn and shipwrecked brother,
Seeing, shall take heart again.

Let us, then, be up and doing,
With a heart for any fate;
Still achieving, still pursuing,
Learn to labour and to wait."

Beware of the Trite—Positive Thinking & Glib Advice

I would not dream of dissing positive thinking; there are too many books written on the subject by professionals smarter than me. But beware, you cannot think your way out of mental illness. I agree with much of what has been written on positive thinking but it is about a mind-set and way of working and approaching problems on a general level. You have to be practised at positive thinking; it's a habit, and it's a skill you can learn. Some of us are better at it than others, by default, genetics or circumstances. I'm a positive thinker and have been glass full all my life. I'm irritatingly positive and that is hard work for the realists and pessimists I engage with. But my positive mind-set did not prevent me from drowning with PTSD. I could not overcome the fear with positive thinking. It's a double-edged sword. I used to remind myself there were others worse off than me; what did I have to be so down about? I'm free, I'm not homeless, I'm not hungry, and I have wonderful friends and a good job. I have so much. But I also have so much fear, too much anxiety, buckets of dread and shed loads of guilt. I couldn't reason these distressing emotions away. I couldn't positively think my way out of PTSD (I had tried and failed).

When someone is in trouble, generally people want to help, and they mean well. But boy do some people say the dumbest of things. My tip is that unless you really have something useful, relevant or insightful to say, keep quiet and listen. At most just admit, 'I can't imagine how that feels' or 'that's not something I have any understanding of' or if you can, and only if you genuinely can, ask, 'is there something I can do to help?'

Please don't tell those of us struggling:

- God only gives these burdens to those that can cope
- Chin up, soldier on, look on the bright side
- Think positive
- Don't dwell on it dear
- Things get better in time
- It's probably hormonal
- Don't worry
- It's your nerves
- You are overthinking this
- Everything always happens for the best

- Give it time, be patient
- Relax
- You'll snap out of it soon
- My aunty, sister, cousin or great-uncle had the same problem and they found herbal tea, vitamin B or turmeric helped
- You don't have enough faith
- If you fight, you can beat this
- It's all in the mind (aka you are making it up)
- Try dating again—a new partner (and sex) might cheer you up
- People have been through far worse
- Get drunk
- Get a dog
- Start running

There were times I couldn't face talking to people. Some people were so stupid and insensitive. Had they listened to what I'd just said? This happened quite a bit in the early days when I was trying to be open about why I was off work or not able to do something normally up my street. I was often shocked and disappointed when people who'd known me for years would try and explain my symptoms away, dismissing them as empty nest syndrome or a menopausal crisis. I wanted to scream when

I heard this crap. I'd been keen for my children to go into the world as soon as it would take them. I had a son who'd walked at nine months and was out exploring before most children were out of nappies. I was the first mum to let her daughter walk to and from school on her own. I had nothing as trivial as empty nest syndrome. As to the menopause, I'd been lucky enough to get that out of the way with no sweat (excuse the pun) in my early forties. I'd been glad to see the back of periods, water retention, swollen breasts and the cruel mood swings of premenstrual tension (PMT), and considered myself perfectly hormonally balanced for the last fifteen years. Good job nobody said such dumb things when I had PMT: now that could have been dangerous for some, I'd have literally bitten heads off back then.

But some people got it right. In the September of 2019, while still off work, I'd been asked to join a local amateur dramatic society as they were putting on a production of Dylan Thomas's Under Milk Wood and my dulcet tones would have lent some authenticity to the show. I explained to the producer that I was interested, but that recently I'd been having days where I was scared of myself and some dark and labile moods. I didn't need to elaborate. This sensitive person kindly suggested I come and see the show (which I did) and consider taking a part another time (which I plan to). This thoughtful person made time just to listen to me, and over the next few months we became friends.

The hashtag (and variations of it) 'it's ok not to be ok'—gets to me. This is in my trite bucket for good reason. #It's ok not to be ok. OK. OK? What do you mean by OK for a start? How can it be OK not to be OK? 'Agahhhhh' give me strength' I scream.

'I am not OK. And it's not OK.'

I am:

Dying inside
Aching
Struggling
Drowning
On the edge
Suffering
Exhausted

Hurting
Falling
Screaming

I am crippled by:

Fear
Anxiety
Anger
Pain
Dread
Loneliness
Self-pity
Guilt
Indecision
Hopelessness

I left OK behind a long time ago. I have PTSD but I'm OK; now that is incongruous. If I'd listened to half the advice given to me by well-meaning folk over the years that I've suffered with PTSD, I'd have become extremely lost and frustrated. Seriously, I know the good intent behind the hash tag 'it's ok not to be ok'; I'm not that naïve. I know in our media hungry world we need simple messages if we are to galvanise change. I get that, I really do. Honest—(drawn out syllables) as we say in Wales. But no more talk, no more empty promises: we need more than talk. We need negotiation and action. I'm not alone in wanting to see that. I'm pleased to see that many more people are now seeking more than a conversation or changing the narrative. They want individuals and organisations doing something to help all of us manage our mental health. Negotiation with ourselves, our families, colleagues, employers, friends, politicians and healthcare providers will enable us to agree what we want and need to stay mentally well. Such a massive negotiation will require creativity, commitment and a changed mind-set from everyone. It will not be easy; I know how hard it was for me to think differently about my mental health and PTSD. We will need courage, and funding, to do something meaningful, especially with the UK GPs' concerns over a surge in PTSD following the Covid-19 pandemic.

Before leaving the topic of positive thinking, it is worth mentioning that there was one feeling I never lost during my journey with PTSD, that of being grateful. It may be that British thing whereby we tend to think 'it could be worse'. I thought that each time I left hospital with one of my kids, I was relieved. It had been worse for some families we'd met in ICU; we'd known children not make it. We'd seen families really struggle with the strain of very sick children. I was grateful for our fortune. I was grateful for the wonderful ambulance crews, doctors and nurses, teachers and our luck. It is hard to describe the uplift, that chink of light of being grateful gave me, and this was all the more magnified during the Covid pandemic. I appreciated that I was alive, with a home, good friends, great kids, fond memories and opportunities for retirement. I live in a country with a wonderful health service and I am free. As the world around me seems to deny so many people some of these things, I took time to reflect on what I had, and said thank you to the wind. I began saying 'thank you', 'that is kind' and 'I love you' whenever there was the chance.

Faith and Mental Health

A truly genuine and faithful colleague (and one in a position of power which meant any disagreement with them would have been awkward), once told me I needed to pray more, to trust in God and lay my burden before him and all would be well. This colleague told me a story about one of his children whose sight had deteriorated due to a serious medical condition: his prayers had been answered with the child having a miraculous recovery and her sight restored. Amazing story and one I believed was true in that something unusual did happen to restore the child's sight, but I did not believe it was due to God's intervention. At this particular time, I was a committed Christian (Baptist to be more specific) and when I heard this, I felt pathetic, unworthy and that my faith must be less than I'd thought it to be, and thus I was less of a Christian than the person before me. I'd never been one to expect God to solve my problems, my faith was based on knowing I had to make an effort myself; I understood that living meant facing painful and unfathomable things. Prayers were not magic wands. I replied rather tersely, and on reflection rudely, 'Thank you for your concern and prayers. However, when the Christians were on their knees in the Roman amphitheatre calling out to God to save them, if I remember correctly, the lions still ate them.'

I've met many people over the years who believe depression is a result of the spiritual shortcomings of the sufferer. Although I've read research showing that faith helps people positively manage their mental health, enlightened people know even the most devout of us require land-based support, possibly alongside spiritual devotions. Clinical diagnosis of a mental health condition requires expert clinical guidance in my book. Period. My mum suffered with depression in her later years, aggravated by ill health and isolation. During that time, we managed to find a super range of good, well-written, sensible, books for her to understand how her faith and depression could co-exist. Taking away the guilt she felt about being depressed enabled my mum to get the support she needed whilst not harming her spiritual well-being.

Over the years my journey into the darkness of PTSD and struggling with the fear following each of the near fatal asthma attacks brought an end to my faith. I'd never felt the promised comfort of a divine hand at any time during the darkness. I never felt uplifted from the bottom of my pit of fear. I never felt a love beyond myself that could sustain me. I only saw blackness, emptiness and isolation. I was alone. I never prayed for God to allow my son to live. I never expected God to give us a 'get out of ITC card'. Life was life and death. I only ever prayed for the comfort of a fatherly God, a comfort that would be shared with my children, husband, my mum and wider family. Nothing came down from the heavens. Much to the sorrow of my mum (whose faith stayed with her right up to her death) I called it a day on being a believer after 25 years of commitment.

Social Media

I don't do it. Never have done. It's not for me or my PTSD.

I was going to leave this bucket as just the sentence above. People tell you, and I agree, that you should never write about what you don't know. I only know that I have never felt the need or desire to spend my time seeking a relationship, or sharing my life over an App or platform. I do not do Facebook, Instagram or Tick Tock. It may be an age thing. I have never needed to be, or feel, included by way of social media. It's not as if all my generation are talking on it. I am not excluded because I don't use it. It is different for the young. I see that. My kids have had to use Facebook for access to university materials. For their generation it is a key communications tool. I only recently put my trust in Google Maps, having found my way around the world with a good paper version; and if I got lost, asking the way. I don't want to be tied to my phone. I don't want to be dependent on gadgets and screens. I want to be self-reliant. Passwords and logins drive me nuts. I have seen so much trite stuff on social media. By way of brevity it is prone to being glib and shallow. There is so much massaging of the stories, so much crafting of the images, that it is hard to know what is real.

At work I used LinkedIn and found this a great way to keep in touch with professional networks and people within my sector. More recently, I have used WhatsApp to great effect since the pandemic. I can talk freely to my friends in India, USA, Switzerland and Scotland. Everything I share is specific and personalised. It's less informal than email and has allowed me to snap quick pictures of me walking, gardening, cooking. I have bored my friends with pictures of my vegan food, my garden harvest and the multicoloured crocheted blankets, hats and ponchos I've made using left over wool. All unedited.

I don't like the disconnection of mainstream social media. I want emotional engagement, response and responsibility from my interactions. I am not convinced social media would give me that. I worry about the 'instantness' of social media; I worry social media makes people impatient, everything has to be looked at now, dealt with now, commented on now. This immediacy feels like pressure to me. I worry that if we use social media too much (and I would not dare to suggest what too much is, but some of the studies suggest 30 minutes a day is sufficient and any more leads to problems) we will lose the skills of face-to-face communications. Reading people is a key skill and I am not so sure you can do that as well via an App. I don't want things filtered, either. I want to choose what I see, and algorithms have no idea what is good for me. My choices are mine and only mine; random, eclectic and private.

I know that social media has its place and can help people with mental health if used in the right way. I don't know what that looks like and so please excuse my brevity on the topic. As my gran used to say, 'if you have nothing useful or kind to say, keep your mouth shut.'

Money Talks

It's not what happens to you but how you chose to deal with events that contribute to the longer-term positive outcomes. I say this very specifically and carefully in relation to traumatic events: we don't choose to witness horrific events, or be the victim of something traumatic. It's not our fault if we are subject to something terrible, unforgettable, unbearable, be it accidental or deliberate. It's not my fault I have PTSD. But part of the problem of PTSD is that although innocent, I feel guilty.

But I have a choice. If the right circumstances are put in place at the right time, I can be free of the guilt. For me it was not at the immediate point of the trauma but much later. I don't have to be defined and confined by the traumatic events of my past. I hold on to the fact that I have choices. I may not be able to see them clearly but I won't be limited by accepting things as just that way. I don't want to live with this much pain and I don't have to accept the disability of my PTSD. I can make decisions that make sense for me and my family; I know I have the capacity, skills, experience, network, intelligence, drive and support to work my way through a problem. But, importantly, I have the financial capacity to support and help myself. This is not the case for many people with mental illness. Choices are not always free. There is a cost to the decisions we have the chance to make, and that cost is often opportunity. Tiresome and cruel as it sounds, 'money does talk'. I'm mentioning this against the backdrop of famous people coming out to talk about mental health. I'm NOT judging. I'm not dissing people for sharing their stories; really, I'm not. It's important we have these stories so we learn to see the signs. It matters that we recognise mental illness can happen to anyone, even the most successful in society, including royalty. Pain is pain whoever you are. Isolation and loneliness can happen to those surrounded by the world and his wife.

I am talking openly and honestly. The plethora of media stories helps me understand why people say 'it's ok not to be ok'. But for many famous people lack of money is not an issue. I'm NOT saying money solves all mental health problems. But most of the time such famous people have access to funds or support to help them deal with their pain and mental illness. They don't have to wait months for an appointment within the NHS. They don't have to wait years to get listened to. They don't have to soldier on waiting to be rescued. When I went to my GP, he openly admitted I would not get seen within the NHS for months, if not longer. I was lucky to have a GP

I had great access to; one I could trust, and who provided instrumental support and advice. That is not always the case for everyone. Many people are not even registered with a GP, and even if they are, they may have had little chance to build a trusting relationship if they have been otherwise healthy. I'm saying living on the street, or in poor housing, with a minimal income coming in, possibly no job, children to take care of, no quick access to good local health services or employers who do not understand, make it almost impossible to help yourself out of the hell in your head. I got out of my hell relatively quickly because I was able to pay for my therapy; my privately paid for counsellor was able to dampen the flames before the PTSD burnt my brain to dust.

I don't want to get political about mental health services and specifically PTSD, the topic is complex and post Covid-19 pandemic the pressures on public health services across the world will be significant. All I do know is that somewhere along the line we have to help ourselves *and* each other. We have to be ready to consider options that allow prompt diagnosis and access to support. I guess this is where charities play a role to an extent. I did not tap into this type of support in part because I did not realise I had PTSD for some time. A friend did suggest I attend a gardening session for people with mental disorders but I declined for three simple reasons. One, I was in no place to expose myself to strangers; I was too scared to meet new people. Two, I was too ashamed; I saw myself as someone who had so much. I had a nice home, a good job, lots of friends and loving children. Three, as awful as this sounds, I didn't want to be surrounded by people with problems. People like me. I didn't want to witness other people's suffering. I had enough shit of my own and I wasn't strong enough, or gracious enough to be civil.

Acceptance that going private may be the way for those with money is not a comprehensive solution but I'm pleased to note that the UK charity MIND does provide guidance on seeking private help and I have not seen this on any other charity site. There is a lot of evidence about the negative impact of mental illness on our economies, societies and health care systems. None of it is inspirational reading, but then I am digging deep into my hope. I want to see and take action for a better place and I hope my scribbles play some small part towards creating a better place for those with PTSD. You know when you were kids on a journey and along the route you'd constantly ask 'are we there yet?' to which the answer was always 'no we have a long way to go yet, be patient troops', I feel like that when I read the reports and policies on mental ill health. Twelve years after a series of reports and recommendations on UK mental ill health were published in 2008 I am asking myself 'are we there yet?' Do we have early identification and intervention as soon as mental health problems emerge? Have we addressed the social determinants and consequences of mental health problems? Has the quality and efficiency of current services improved?

I'm not sure we can expect any health service alone to be solely responsible for the solutions. Our UK NHS can't be expected to address the pandemic of mental health issues it seems to be facing, especially post Covid. But we have to remember the right choices are all too often a luxury. We can contribute to maintaining good mental health if we take a shared responsibility. I suggest we start being accountable for mental health on individual, familial, corporate and societal levels. Not an easy task.

Mind over Matters—Matters over Mind

Being an optimist, I believe we can care for ourselves and others if we have access to the right insight, support and services. I doubt we can prevent PTSD from happening: people will always face trauma of some kind and we can't prevent such events happening. Events we witness or are the subject of (as civilians outside of war), including rape, child abuse, horrific accidents, traumatic crime, death and near death. Neither can we control or predict how people will respond to traumatic events; we are all unique. But I do believe we can better prepare ourselves to deal with PTSD once it kicks. We can limit the damage and disability PTSD causes. If we put our mind to it, we can make things better, sooner. If we work collectively, we can:

Recognise PTSD earlier
Diagnose PTSD quicker
Improve access to care
Make intelligent holistic decisions about medication
Remove mental health inequalities

Help sufferers to help themselves
Monitor PTSD over time

PTSD is not a condition you can solve just by the pre-scription of medication. Medication did help me. With-out it I'd have been stuck for a very long time in my pit of despair. It prevented me from being harmed further by PTSD. It kept me from drowning and helped me to survive. However, medication did not help me thrive. To do that I had to work hard; I had to take the support and love of friends and family; I had to trust my GP and ther-apist; I had to scrutinise myself during CBT; and most painfully, I had to feel during EMDR. I had to feel cou-rageous in the face of pain and fear. That was hard work; bloody hard work.

My thoughts and feelings are not facts. It's difficult, but not impossible, to measure how we feel. My thoughts and feelings are not visible, tangible; they don't translate into data readily and are not transferrable or analysable. What we see is actually our responses to our thoughts and feelings; we see tears, smiles, laughter, self-harm, suicide, violence and substance abuse. We see the consequence of our thoughts and feeling in our actions. And so, what mental illness looks like is important; this is why I decided to share my story, to help us see pain, fear and distress.

PTSD caused me to behave in a certain way: I was acting differently to 'normal', acting in more ways than one. People who helped me come through PTSD saw the signs, and stepped in to help. They reacted in the right way. They did not ignore me or dismiss the signs. They talked to me and they listened to me. It was that simple.

In the UK we have been aware of health inequality for some years and with the increased awareness of mental health the time is upon us to have a constructive dialogue. The dialogue will need to be holistic as the strands are many and complex; circumstances, culture, environment, and motivation all have a part to play. I know many people with mental health needs do not have the supportive structures I had access to and this is something I'd like to see addressed in the conversations going on, especially following the Covid-19 pandemic. I don't have the answers, I only have words. My words may be the catalyst for someone with PTSD to have the most important conversation of all, that of asking for help. The next important conversation is how to share the provision and responsibility of that help. There are ways out of PTSD; you have to start with recognising you have it, and how bad you have it, and that is not as easy as it sounds.

Therapy is:

Essential
Catalytic
A buoyancy aid
Hard work
Personal
Life changing

Medication is:

Optional
Temporary
Helpful
Distilling
Balancing
Stabilising
Considered OK

Support is:

A cornerstone
Healing
Patient
Understanding
Non-judgemental
Good
Honest
Strong

Resilience—Where'd You Get It?

At the end of one of my sessions with my therapist in early 2020 she mentioned talking about my case with her boss, who was curious as to my resilience. I stifled a laugh at the question. I took a deep breath and gave a whistle-stop tour of my life from middle school to middle age. When I'd first met my therapist in Oxford in the autumn of 2019, I confined my history to the last decade or so, those since 2001 when I'd first witnessed my son's bad asthma attack. I believed there was enough to talk through without looking any further back. But I realise I am who I am because of the tapestry of my past:

The good and the bad,
The ups and the downs,
The happy and horrid,
The love and the hate,
The bliss and the strife,
The laughter and the tears,
The joy and the sadness,
The bitter and the sweet,
The right and the wrong,
The success and failures,

The living and the dead,
The light and the dark.

How did I acquire my resilience? Or more bluntly put, how did I learn to shovel the shit that came my way and still smile? I've experienced my fair share of troubles and life events, growing up in a dysfunctional family, studying at Leeds University when Peter Sutcliffe was murdering young women, having an appendectomy whilst visiting Cyprus, malignant melanoma when pregnant, breaking my collar bone playing rounders, delivering my 2nd child unexpectedly at home, and living with an alcoholic husband. Both my children had significant health problems when growing up. Apart from his asthma, my youngest battled with ADHD; he was also hospitalised for a terrible bout of Henoch-Schonlein purpura (HSP), acute pancreatitis and major surgery to repair a tear to his thigh (after ripping his leg open on barbed wire). My daughter got dealt a bum set of genes, suffering lactose intolerance, a severe nut allergy, asthma, eczema, repeated bouts of tonsillitis, recurrent infections, IBS and molar incisor hypomineralisation (MIH), which resulted in four molar teeth being removed when she was only six. In her early twenty's epilepsy was added to the list.

Over the years we'd had many a cancelled holiday because of hospital admissions, six holidays in total. The first holiday denied us was a trip to South Africa, all carefully planned as not to be far away from a hospital or medical facility (yes, we planned all our holidays around knowing where the local hospitals were). That year the kids had researched all the wildlife we would see and been given South African Rands as an early Christmas present by my mum. Our bags were packed and we knew our route off by heart. Then three days before we were due to leave my sons' asthma kicked off and we spent the next week hoping he would live. We came home from hospital on Christmas Eve. We had nothing prepared for Christmas. Within a few hours of being home we managed to rush around our local shops and get basic supplies for Christmas day; a turkey from our butcher minutes before his shop closed, all the trimmings and even some token presents. Clever Santa. It was one of the best Christmases we had as a family; we were just glad our boy was alive and celebrated that with immense relief. Ever since then we don't overdo or over spend at Christmas; we keep it very simple, focusing on the time we spend with each other.

We became adept at insurance claims. If you need to know which are the best travel insurance companies, I'm the one to ask. Some companies were brilliant, efficient and empathetic; others were a pain in the arse and made us jump through hoops to get the holiday refunded, making us feel like beggars. In fact, my first bad experience with travel insurance followed the first near fatal event, whilst on holiday in Guernsey. We were due to travel home on the ferry the day of the trauma and thank god we did not get on the boat or it would have been a different outcome. I can't tell you the pressure I felt to just get home; not getting on the ferry and getting to hospital was the only sensible thing to do. Naturally we had to find accommodation while my son was in hospital and that in itself was a palaver as it was the August Bank holiday. The hospital put me up in the junior doctors' quarters so I could be near, and my husband and daughter managed to find a room in the hotel a few yards from the hospital. When we came to claim, the insurance company denied forking out for my husband and daughter. They claimed that they should have got on the ferry to go home, leaving me and 'the patient' on the island. I took the claim to appeal and the ombudsman and won. We had super help from the ferry company; when we explained our predicament, they gave us new tickets with priority boarding for the eventual return home and charged us no extra. The insurance company only had to pay for the cost of four nights in a hotel for one adult as the hotel had also been understanding and not charged for my seven-year-old daughter. There were times we could not get travel insurance at a cost we could afford. Travel to the USA was out of the question, and some European travel policy quotes were more than the cost of the holiday. So, we went to Wales a lot.

Getting a diagnosis of cancer is no fun. Getting a diagnosis of cancer when you are pregnant is shocking. Before I fell pregnant with my 2nd child, we'd moved house and as part of getting a new mortgage I'd been asked to go for a medical. I duly trotted off to see a doctor in Oxford; a stereotypical overweight, waist coated, red nosed old-fashioned GP, in dark velvet wall papered rooms off the Woodstock Road. I bounced in expecting to pass with flying colours. The GP agreed to sign me off as fit, but…… He asked me to lose weight and get a dark freckle along my bra line examined by a specialist. I was furious; how dare he comment on my weight. I was well covered and had not absolutely lost the weight from my first child. Hump.

A few months later, after we moved house, my husband reminded me about the dark freckle on my back. I agreed to get it looked at, mainly because by now my father had died an awful death from recurrent malignant melanoma. My GP did not hesitate to refer me and I was seen quickly by the specialist dermatology team. At the time, I was most worried about a large mole that had appeared almost overnight, right slap bang in the middle of my pubic area. I couldn't see the dark freckle on my back as it was along my bra line, an impossible place to view. The dermatology team reassured me that it was unlikely either blemish was anything to worry about. After all I had freckles on every bit of my fair body, but best to be sure. They agreed to excise tissue for examination from my back and remove the mole in my private parts completely. They agreed to do this there and then. I had gone to the clinic on my own, driven there on the way home from work. Big mistake. It was summer and I was wearing loose fitting clothes and cami-knickers. After the minor surgery I headed for home, but the walk to the car park was tricky. The dressing on my pubic area was falling down my legs and I felt very faint. I hobbled to the hospital League of Friends café, fuelled myself with sweet tea and waited an hour or so. I hesitantly drove home; feeling rather silly for not thinking ahead.

A couple of days later the results came back. The mole was nothing to worry about but the innocuous freckle turned out to be malignant melanoma. It was the middle of August 1996 and I'd just had a positive a pregnancy test, my second child was due in the spring of 1997.

Not good timing. My GP, the dermatologist and plastic surgeons were a wonderful support and I had further surgery immediately to excise the melanoma. I have had no further troubles with melanoma but over the years I did regularly have freckles and blemishes removed, some of which were solar keratosis and basal cell carcinomas (BCC). Caught early BCC can be removed readily. To this day I am religious about checking my skin, as none of the blemishes, other than the fanny mole, were obvious; the dangerous ones were subtle and sinister.

Diversion but relevant addition….

Years later at one of my regular dermatology check-ups, I had a red blemish on my shoulder. I was being examined by the medical students and naked except for my pants I was flushed and embarrassed. The consultant asked me to try to stop blushing and to do this he asked me to think of something sad. I thought of those bad asthma attacks; it worked. I went as a pale as a winter's moon. I admitted my technique to the observing students who were surprised at the colour transformation. Chameleon Me. Once I was back to my normal pale self the red mark on my shoulder was quite obvious. It was agreed I would come back the next day, with my husband, to get a biopsy. The next morning I woke up to find my whole body covered in hundreds of red rings. It looked like some enthusiastic child had been having fun with a red felt tip pen or potato printing. I flashed my body at my husband and we both knew immediately that I had a bad case of ring worm. I was covered from head to foot in perfect rings, back and front. We went to the dermatology clinic as planned and the diagnosis was confirmed. No one had spotted it was potentially ringworm the previous day. Thank goodness they didn't do a biopsy that day. Ringworm is highly infectious. The medical students were asked to suggest a treatment and some bright spark suggest prescribing antifungal cream. It would have taken hundreds of 30 mg tubes of antifungal creams to treat me. I ended up on antifungal tablets for a few weeks; the consultant warned me that the antifungal medication had a negative impact on the contraceptive pill and to take extra precautions. As if anyone would want sex with a highly infectious, red blotched, woman who was constantly itching. My husband certainly had no intention of making a move in that direction, and for his safety and that of my daughter I was confined to sleeping alone.

On a Thursday one summer as I was turning fifty, I broke my collar bone playing rounders. I was on a team building picnic with my colleagues. I was meant to be watching as I'm not one for ball games and I'd not done any running for some years. But because of the pressure from the young'uns, I joined in. First time in batting I slogged the ball way into the field, much to my surprise. It went so far I thought I'd be able to walk to 4th base, but as one of the fielding team raced to the ball I decided to trot for a rounder. I was trotting from 2nd to 3rd base when I stumbled on a tuft of grass. I rolled, got up and jogged on to score. I was mildly pleased. The team changed over and I was asked to man 4th base. It was as the ball was heading my way and I went to lift my arm to catch it that a searing pain ran through my body. Such acute and excruciating agony across my collar bone and rib cage nearly made me faint. I missed the ball and quietly made excuses to sit down. I thought I must have twisted something when I stumbled. Time came to pack up and I was in agony. I used my right hand to direct everyone to put all the stuff in the boot of my car. I sat for a while in the driving seat trying to relax. I waited for everyone to leave and then took a deep breath and started the car. As I moved my left hand to put the car into first gear the pain in my arm ripped into my being. I actually screamed. I had not screamed like that giving birth. I drove home in first gear for 27 miles. How the hell I managed to get through traffic lights and take turnings safely I have no idea. I could not change gear or signal. It was a bloody stupid and dangerous thing to do. In defence of my actions, we were in an area with no phone signal and it was pre my smart phone days. It took me 2 hours to do a 40-minute journey, I got home in tears. I assumed I had twisted something. The next day, Friday, I insisted on going to work as I had a big training day arranged for my team with an eminent expert lined up for the day. It was hard work getting ready as it hurt to move my left arm. My husband drove me to work and we planned to take me to A&E later in the day. The time came to go to A&E and by now I was tired and I was concerned that we had not finished packing for our summer holiday. On Saturday we were flying to the island of São Miguel in the Azores. The thought of A&E on a Friday evening was enough to put me off despite the agony I was in. I once again directed operations with my right hand and we managed to get to the Azores. That night, settled in our hotel getting ready for bed, as we all struggled to help me get out of my clothes the severe bruising across my left side became apparent, as was a bone sticking up across my collar area. We realised then I had broken something. The kids had iPads and looked up remedies for a broken collar bone and thus the next morning we drove to the local town, Ponta Delgada, to find a pharmacy to buy a sling. As it turned out the shop we found was owned by a pharmacist who also ran the archipelago's disability shop.

I was marched around to said shop; amid bath hoists, wheelchairs, and toilet frames I was fitted out with a top of the range brace for my broken collar bone. A navy-blue brace, my holiday souvenir. We had a super holiday even though doing some things, such as swimming with dolphins in the Atlantic Ocean was out of the question.

On returning to the UK, I went to A&E and got a bit of a telling off; doctors hate dealing with old injuries and by now it had been ten days since the rounder's incident. At first the doctor doubted I had done any major damage but duly sent me off for an X-ray. When the results confirmed I had indeed broken my collar bone, the doctor was aghast and asked why I had given the injury a pain score of 7. Apparently grown men, rugby players, jockeys and bikers alike (sports prone to collar bone breakages) tend to rate such pain as 10. Easy answer; Pain is relative, cluster headaches—10, first child no painkillers 9, second child no pain killers 8—broken collar bone 7, with acute appendicitis and inner ear infection 6.

There was a silver (pun intended) lining to breaking my bones. As I was fifty, I was duly sent for further tests to rule out osteoporosis. I felt like a fraud as I raced (as I was invariably late from trying to find a parking space) into the clinic at the local hospital. As I sat with silver-haired elderly patients who invariably had Zimmer frames, signs of incontinence, hearing aids and support tights, I cringed with embarrassment and a degree of sadness (this would be me one day), confident my skeleton was healthy and strong. I was quite wrong. I had osteopenia in my spine, no doubt the consequence of an early menopause and a strong family history of osteoporosis. Thanks to breaking my collar bone I was able to access early treatment to prevent further bone loss and problems with broken bones. I am humbled by this experience and vow not to diss the elderly any further. I consider myself a resilient person. I have a way of dealing with dilemmas that usually works. Part of my coping is to remind myself of what I have, and how lucky I am that things aren't worse. When my good friend and I were reminiscing about the impact of her breast cancer and my malignant melanoma on our lives, it prompted my line, 'at least I still have my own teeth, my own hair and my own tits, which is more than you can say' The grass was greener on my side. I was lucky. That's how I saw it. My glass is always half full.

Quitting Work

When all is said and done, I had an extremely rewarding career; I travelled widely, met interesting people, solved no end of problems, built up businesses including one of my own, and learnt much along the way. When I first went into the workplace there was no internet, computers or mobile phones; we used pen and paper and the post office to send messages; we talked to people on the phone or in meetings; we read books and talked to experts as part of finding stuff out (research) and we had secretaries and tea trollies. Time flies and thirty-five years on as I write this bucket, I have a phone that allows me to talk freely to the world, research a question in minutes, take great photographs and book a flight or buy anything from seeds to cars. But time is still time and very precious, because you're not guaranteed to have it; you never know when your time will run out. Bit profound and thinking too much about the concept of time can drive you nuts, but I pondered a lot about time during the lockdown months of 2020. Time has given me memories. They are my memories; my time.

You can't buy time.
You can't sell time.

You can't borrow time.
You can't make time.
You can't take time.

You can't make time but you can make memories, and it was with this in mind that I thought about my future; my future with PTSD and my future without PTSD. How would I get from one place to the other? What memories do I want to create with whatever time I have at my disposal? I realised I was trying to get to a place with my PTSD that would allow me to return to work. It was as if this was the measure by which I would know I was right (better, stronger, or cured). But the attempt to go back to work had shown me that the environment was not conducive for someone senior like me with a serious mental health issue and by the spring of 2020 I was months into being off sick, and facing the prospect of statutory sick pay. I wanted to be free of the label of being 'off-sick'; I wanted to stop getting sick notes and reporting back to strangers on how I was doing. I wanted to get stronger at my pace and focus on surviving the Covid pandemic. I spoke with my family and close friends and eventually decided to step out of corporate life. It was a scary call and a decision I did not make lightly; I was, after all, in the middle of a divorce, nearly sixty and the country was in lockdown with little idea of what the future would hold. I wanted to live a different life; one that would allow me to focus on me; a life that would allow me to evolve and make memories and new friends and ditch PTSD. By lockdown I knew three things: one, writing was helping me heal; two, I had to thrive despite the curveball of Covid; three, I was in no fit state to return to work. I needed to take a risk; I had to trust myself. I had to try to move the dial, back the odds in my favour and increase my chances of thriving. I was not going to give up or give in to PTSD. In April 2020 I stopped work.

As Lucio says in Shakespeare's Measure for Measure, 'Our doubts are traitors and make us lose the good we oft might win by fearing to attempt.' If I had been younger, my decision to stop work would certainly have been different; stopping work would not have been financially viable. It would have been impossible and not the right thing to do for a woman in her professional prime, especially one who was paying the mortgage. By 2020 I was in a financial position that allowed me to consider stepping out of paid employment. I was also, at nearly sixty, not far off a tidy retirement age. My experience with PTSD in the work place had led me to wonder if corporations, insurance companies and senior management have the skills, tools and policies to support those with longer term mental health issues, especially those at a senior level. I know I felt vulnerable, confused about my rights and disadvantaged by being out of the office off sick with a long-term mental health issue. I experienced a lot of ignorance about PTSD in the corporate setting. Our health services and the armed forces have resources and people ready to deal with PTSD specifically. Such support services can be adapted for conversations about mental health in more corporate and commercial environments; the jury is out on whether this is working or happening to date. I have not regretted stopping work. Not one single bit. It has been a critical step in my recovery from PTSD. I am evolving in more ways than I could ever have imagined, despite the horror and restrictions of Covid-19. I am working on myself these days and that's hard enough work for now. Having time to thrive, and not just survive, has been critical to my recovery.

The C-word

COVID-19 has been cruel. Cruel to individuals, families, communities and businesses. Viruses are insidious, we can't see them, we can't smell them, we can't touch them (not that we would want to). The end of my story would have been different had the Covid pandemic not taken hold in early 2020. In the spring of 2020, I believed I had made decent progress with getting out of the PTSD pit. I knew I had some way to go and I expected ups and downs. I expected hurdles, challenges and setbacks. I did not expect a pandemic. PTSD and pandemics are not good bedfellows. I was going to have to dig deep to withstand the onslaught of anxiety. Never before had the word resilience meant so much. During 2020 I watched our language change; our vocabulary was full of new and negatives concepts. We were surrounded by death and destruction, of people, of businesses and of livelihoods. I wanted to hibernate. Come out of my burrow when the air was clean and the streets busy, the pubs full, the markets bustling, with children playing noisily in the parks.

Covid-cases
Hospital admissions

R rate
Lockdown
Tiers
Isolation
Quarantine
Shielding
Testing
PPE
Masks
1st wave
2nd wave
3rd wave
Social distancing
Washing hands
2M apart
Vulnerable
ICU
Vaccine
Travel corridors
Variant
Mutation
Trace
Roadmap
Body bags
Deaths

Deaths
Deaths

Towards the end of January 2021, we were seeing higher deaths in the UK, more than in the spring of 2020. As the number of deaths reported for England reached 82,000, and global deaths, 2 million, I found it hard to stay positive. The numbers were becoming unreal, a blur. The numbers reflected broken dreams, lost loved ones and unfinished lives. The TV was awash with scenes of hectic intensive care units, tired nurses, exhausted doctors, crying relatives, and scared patients. I felt weighed down by the misery but I also felt grateful that to date I had not been directly touched by the bloody, cruel virus. I held on to that feeling of thankfulness, day by day I reminded myself of this. Teeth, Hair and Tits, and no Covid.

During the pandemic, routine helped me cope. Cope in general, and cope with the PTSD. When the pandemic kicked off in 2020, I estimated that we could be dealing with the fallout for up to two years. This was the realist in me coming out; this was me bookending the problem. I knew I would need stamina to cope. I would need to pace myself and help my children-young-adults do the same. I told myself and my offspring to set realistic goals, as we had to just get through this. We had to protect ourselves physically and mentally. We were going to have to work hard to stay alive and sane. Being couped up, isolated, and estranged from friends' and family was going to take its toll. We had to be ready for this. We had to prepare. We had to take some control over our restricted lives. Good old routine. Eat breakfast lunch and dinner, exercise, plan the day, talk to family and friends on the phone two to three times a week, cook new meals, make jam, garden, cathartic cleaning, write, rest, walk and talk, read, listen to music and podcasts, learn a new skill (crocheting for me), watch the BBC news at 6 or the Channel 4 news at 7, and Andrew Marr on Sunday mornings. I did wish I could sing during these times; I was inspired by all the online choirs but being a realist, I declined to join one when asked.

This routine was not about me avoiding dealing with my anxiety, dread, depression or fear, or being controlling; it was important to me to keep being me, to keep trying, to help myself. I know well enough that exercise, diet and learning new skills are great ways to stay physically and mentally healthy. As the nation struggled to deal with a pandemic of mental illness, the TV was awash during the Covid crisis with programmes on the benefits of walking, dancing, doing puzzles, and eating special/well balanced diets. I did find this sort of sad, that it took a pandemic to persuade some people to do the right things to maintain their well-being but then I caught myself. Who was I to judge? Doing the right thing is not always obvious or possible; I had learnt that. External help and catalysts are key and I applauded the TV producers for a wonderful mix of self-help telly.

One of my indicators of struggling is the manifestation of overdoing it. My daughter became my manic-monitor, helping me switch off, go slow and re-pace. I think of this in the same way as lifesaving: when you are drowning one of the worst things you can do is waste energy on swimming, you will increase your chances of survival if you float. Keep calm, relax and lay on the surface of the water. This is not easy. It requires a lot of you when you are scared, and the waves are crashing around you, when you are cold and can't see the shore. Waiting for people like me is a big ask. My CBT training had taught me to be still and this pandemic was going to test these newly acquired skills. I spent hours laying on my lounge floor emptying my head of all the turmoil; I did yoga with my daughter, and in the wonderfully hot summer I lay in a kiddie paddling pool sipping homemade lemonade. I was aware by now that even being able to do these things was something to be thankful for. Garden apartheid was apparent; my access to a garden, fresh air and privacy was not something I took for granted anymore. Grateful? Yessiree.

Dead
Death
Dead
Death

Covid-19 kills

Kills
Kills
Kills

I hate funfairs and theme parks; I can't stand rides and rollercoasters; on the rare occasions I have been forced on a ride, I have either been sick and/or wet myself. I am pathologically frightened of most of Thorpe Park and even much of Legoland. When working in Pharma I regularly attended the annual European Respiratory Society meetings. One year the conference was held in Vienna, Austria. My colleagues and I took the chance one evening to go to the oldest amusement park in the world, Wurstelprater. I had no intention of going on any scary rides, a demure carousel was more my plan. You know what's coming. Peer pressure and being plugged with two glasses of wine I was 'forced' on one of the parks famous wooden rollercoasters. I shared the ride with one of my team, a big and easy-going chap; being wedged in the carriage made me feel a little safer. The ride started and before we even came to any speed or rise, I had my eyes closed and was screaming for blue murder. I hated every minute of it, my stomach lurched into my skull, my bladder lost all muscle tone and my nerves were shredded like woodwool. When the ride stopped my colleagues had to lift me out of the ride as I was holding on so tight to the handrail that all my muscles were fixed, gripped by terror. I was shaking and crying. It was and wasn't funny. A few days later when we were all back in the office my colleague with whom I shared the ride was wearing a short-sleeved shirt at our weekly catch-up meeting; I commented on the bruises on his right arm. I was ashamed to learn the crime was mine—not only had I gripped him so hard to cause this harm but on lifting his sleeve up teeth marks were evident. I had been so frightened I had bitten down into his arm to stem my fear. The injury took a lot of explaining to his fiancé. Who would believe, 'my boss did this'?

I digress with this tale as during the pandemic people aptly described the pandemic as being on a roller-coaster. For me this made sense—one hell of a scary ride—one that you cannot get off whilst it is going—one that will shake you up. Highs, lows, action, lulls, relief, coping, struggling, laughing, crying, hoping, criticising, anger, forgiveness, thanks, cruelty, kindness, bored, busy, duty-bound, courage, exhaustion, careful, reckless, lock-down, no lock-down, loss, gain, dying, recovering, and so much bloody waiting. Waiting for the end of the pandemic, Waiting for the vaccine. Waiting to be free. Waiting for the fear to dispel. Waiting for safety.

Covid and PTSD Diary 2020

January

3rd: Qasem Soleimani, one of Iran's most senior military figures is killed in a US drone strike.

8th: A Ukraine International Airlines (UIA) flight shot down by the Iranian Islamic Revolutionary Guards Corp (IRGC) shortly after taking off from Tehran, kills all 176 passengers and crew members on board.

9th: Australia fights one of its worst bushfire seasons, fuelled by record-breaking temperatures and months of severe drought, to date at least 25 people have died and thousands made homeless.

18th: Buckingham Palace confirm that Harry and Megan, the Duke and Duchess of Sussex, will no longer be senior working royals.

20th: The WHO confirm first cases of Covid-19 infection outside mainland China, in Japan, South Korea and Thailand.

23rd: Wuhan (population over 11 million) is cut off by the Chinese authorities due to an alarming rise in Covid-19 infection.

31st: The first two cases of coronavirus in the UK confirmed. The Wellcome Trust calls the coronavirus a 'significant and urgent threat to global health'. Globally, 213 people dead and 9,800 infected.

At this stage I am not too alarmed; it seemed inevitable the virus would get to the UK due to international travel. I felt sure the UK government and health system would knock it on the head soon enough.

Tried going back to work after a shit Christmas only to realise that I was nowhere near well enough to return to work. It seemed the medication was helping but I was crippled by indecision, anxiety, mood swings and depression. I wanted to avoid everyone and everything. I needed to hide away, I needed to stop. I needed to be kind to myself. I needed to accept my limitations at this time. I acknowledged I was sick but some days still found it hard to accept 'this weakness, this PTSD'. I spent January walking and talking with my daughter and making sure I was keeping up on my mindfulness and CBT practices. I was sure by mid-year I could be out of the pit of PTSD.

February

6th: A third case of coronavirus confirmed in the UK. Two avalanches strike a Turkish mountainside, killing 41 people and injuring 84.

8th & 9th: Storm Ciara hits the UK causing severe flooding and three deaths, followed a week later by storm Dennis which causes further damage and five more deaths.

23rd: 13 cases of coronavirus in the UK.

24th: Katherine Johnson, the mathematical genius who enabled NASA to send men to the moon (portrayed in the 2016 film Hidden Figures) dies at the age of 101.

28th: First British death from Covid confirmed by the Japanese Health Ministry; a man quarantined on the cruise ship Diamond Princess.

29th: Man in Surrey infected with COVID-19 despite not having recently travelled abroad.

I am coming towards the end of EMDR therapy. Each session is exhausting and I feel so fragile, so untogether, so shaken. My flashbacks have stopped and I have less nightmares. But my fear and anxiety still hem me in. Sadness sticks to me, like dog poo on shoes, never quite able to get rid of it no matter how hard you try.

March

5th: First death from coronavirus in the UK confirmed, with 115 people having tested positive.

8th: Third death from coronavirus reported in Manchester, and the number of cases in the UK rises to 273.

9th: My last EMDR session.

11th: Film producer Harvey Weinstein sentenced in the US to 23 years in prison for rape and sexual assault.

12th: The FTSE 100 plunges by over 10%, its biggest drop since 1987. Markets around the world are negatively affected by ongoing economic turmoil, in part due to Covid.

17th: NHS England announces the postponement of all non-urgent operations in England to free up hospital beds to accommodate COVID-19 patients.

19th: Bank of England cuts interest rates to 0.1%, the lowest in the Bank's 325-year history.

22nd: Mother's Day.

23rd: In a televised address, Boris Johnson announces a UK-wide partial lockdown, in an effort to contain the spread of the virus. Worldwide figures stand at more than 270,000 cases and 11,000 deaths.

24th: For the first time, all the UK's mobile networks send out a government text alert, ordering people to stay at

home. The message reads: 'GOV.UK CORONAVI-
RUS ALERT. New rules in force now: you must stay
at home. More info and exemptions at gov.uk/coro-
navirus Stay at home. Protect the NHS. Save lives.'

26th: Lockdown Regulations come into effect, which
include significant restrictions on freedom of movement: 'no person may leave the place where they are
living without reasonable excuse'. Clap for Carers is
kicked off by Annemarie Plas and we join our street
in banging pots and clapping at 8pm.

30th: One of my favourite singers Bill Withers, best known
for the 1970s hits Lean on Me, Lovely Day and Ain't
No Sunshine, dies age 81 from heart complications.

31st: Number new daily cases for the UK, 4515, deaths
403.

The London Marathon cancelled and Tokyo Olympics
are postponed.

I was beginning to unravel. My nightmares have returned
and I am screaming in my sleep. I wake up with the dread.
I feel the dark cloak heavy on my shoulders. I dread my
kids will get Covid and die. The pain in my chest returns
as does my IBS. I am chewing my gum shield to bits at
night. I can feel a tsunami of anxiety flooding thorough

my body. I keep to my mantra and invoke my new skills but I feel shit scared again.

On Friday 20th March, my son came home for Mother's Day weekend and by then the UK Covid-19 cases had increased to 3269 people with 144 patients confirmed dead. Over the weekend we talked and I realised we were all shit scared, all three of us. I recognised the fear in my children's faces and voices. We all felt the same. Recognising this shared fear was a critical moment and made me realise that not only did I have a lot more unfinished business with the PTSD, but that also that my children had their own demons to wrestle with.

I can't help but see silver linings and after our tearful discussions about the potential impact of the pandemic on their health, we moved onto reflecting how the past had shaped us. We knew we were a resilient family, not one to dwell on past shit, or let misfortunate deny us our ambitions, but it was evident we were all carrying a burden. The aftermath of those life-threatening attacks was guilt, confusion, pain, abandonment, anxiety and blankness. Covid opened another Pandora's box. At least now we were all on the same page, sharing our fears has helped us all move forward in a good way; the transparency allowing us to support each other with insight, as three adults: mother, daughter, son, brother, sister.

April

April fool's day: 672 Covid deaths in the UK. The 26th session of the Conference of the Parties (COP26), the major UN climate summit, due to be held in Glasgow in November 2020, is postponed to 2021 due to the COVID-19 pandemic. Wimbledon cancelled due to Covid.

3rd: Coronavirus confirmed global cases pass one million.

5th: Prime Minister Boris Johnson gets admitted to hospital with coronavirus infection. The Queen makes a broadcast to the UK and the wider Commonwealth, thanking people for following the government's social distancing rules; she pays tribute to key workers, and says the UK 'will succeed' in its fight against the epidemic but may have 'more still to endure'.

10th: Number of confirmed deaths worldwide from Covid passes 100,000.

15th: UK Health Secretary announces new guidelines that allows close family members to see dying relatives to say goodbye to them. In the US President Donald Trump cuts off U.S. support for the World Health Organization, even as the death rate from the coronavirus pandemic accelerates, with worldwide confirmed deaths topping 127,000.

22ⁿᵈ: UK human COVID-19 vaccine trials start.

25ᵗʰ: Worldwide COVID-19 deaths reach 200,000.

29ᵗʰ: Irrfan Khan, the actor from the films *Slumdog Millionaire* and *Life of Pi* dies in Mumbai of cancer.

30ᵗʰ: 634 Covid deaths in the UK.

It was the sunniest April on record for the UK as a whole.

I am still unravelling. The next few weeks into April were awful. I was spinning out of control. I had a telephone session with my therapist mid-month and this helped. She provided me with additional self-help materials on relapse, which immediately helped me shed the guilt that had been creeping back. Looking on the bright side, I was thankful that by the time the pandemic hit us and lock-down was called, I had completed my EMDR therapy. Covid-19 was going to be tough and I needed to withstand the uncertainty of the coming months. I had the tools to survive. But would I be able to use them in the face of this unprecedented pandemic?

As Ennis Del Mar, a man of few words, says at the end of the film (the last line written by Annie Proulx) of that great story of stoicism, *Brokeback Mountain*:

'There was some open space between what he knew and what he tried to believe, but nothing could be done about it, and if you can't fix it, you've got to stand it.'

I stopped work.

May

1st: 6403 people die of Covid globally.

9th: Little Richard, the self-proclaimed "architect of rock 'n' roll", dies age of 87.

25th: George Floyd, a 46-year-old African-American, died on a pavement in Minneapolis after being handcuffed and brutally pinned to the ground under the knee of a white police officer for more than nine minutes; the terrible scene was shared on social media, stimulating peoples across the globe to support Black Lives Matter.

26th: Global worldwide COVID-19 cases pass 5.5 million.

30th: Elon Musk's company SpaceX is the first commercial operator to carry astronauts into space (in a rocket ship named Dragon) under a public-private partnership set up by NASA.

31st: 60 Covid deaths today, 1069 new cases, UK.

I found the latter weeks of lock-down weirdly peaceful. I had licence to hide, licence to stay in my bubble, permission to keep away from people, shops, traffic, and normal life. I was staying safe in more ways than the government slogan had meant. Knowing my children were also locked down and taking the government advice very seriously I started to feel comfortable.

Comfortable with being hidden away.
Comfortable with being confined to my home.
Comfortable keeping away from people.
Comfortable with lockdown.

It was disconcerting how quickly I'd become comfortable and adept with the quarantine we were obliged to keep. I wanted to live like this forever, shielding for life. I set to sewing batches of face masks for family and friends. First batch was too big as I used an American pattern and they ended up looking like neck braces. Second batch was perfect as face masks were established as a pandemic essential, and the most politicised accessory of the decade.

Twelve weeks into lockdown, my son had to make a difficult decision, that of returning to work. He'd been furloughed but like many small businesses (2-man band) it was make or break time. Although we were all concerned about his returning to work, it was apparent that his anxiety was becoming disabling and he was subtly becoming phobic of going anywhere. His mental health was my main concern. We examined the risks; he lived in an area with a low infection rate; he worked outdoors; he worked in protective gear anyway; and he worked mainly with one guy, his boss (who was being careful as he had elderly family). His going back to work proved the right call: being physical and mentally active, and engaging, albeit at a distance, with people buoyed his spirits and the bank balance.

June

5th: The WHO calls for nations to encourage the increased use of face mask coverings.

15th: Bob Dylan releases his 39th album, 'Rough and Rowdy Ways', a batch of great new songs for 8 years.

20th: Greta Thunberg says the world must learn lessons from the pandemic and treat climate change with a similar urgency.

23rd: 94 people die in the UK, on my birthday. President Trump extends and expands visa restrictions temporarily suspending some work visas and barring more than 500,000 foreigners from entering the US. Saudi Arabia announces that the annual hajj pilgrimage to

Mecca will be limited to people already living in the kingdom because of the coronavirus pandemic. Tennis world number one Novak Djokovic tests positive for coronavirus.

28th: Confirmed global coronavirus cases hit 10 million as death toll passes 500,000.

30th: 53 deaths, 403 new cases UK. China passes a new security law in Hong Kong, criminalising any act of secession, subversion, terrorism or collusion with foreign forces.

Months into the pandemic, like many people I felt an insidious agoraphobia taking hold. My daughter and I had been shielding now for months, and when the time came to venture out it felt like stepping into battle. I WAS NERVOUS. The armour of the face masks and the strategy of social distancing serving to quicken my pulse, making me confused and sweaty. I took to only going out to public places with my daughter; a comfort for each other.

I started buying flour in 16 kg sacks to make our own bread. Sorted the attic and cupboards out just like the rest of the nation. Agreed with Greta and made a concerted effort to buy less food wrapped in plastic.

July

4th: 32 deaths, 624 new cases UK.

17th: 100-year-old Captain Sir Tom Moore knighted by the Queen for raising more than £32m for NHS charities by walking more than 100 laps of his garden.

18th: 9 deaths, 827 new cases UK.

24th: wearing of face coverings compulsory in shops and supermarkets in England.

30th: 0 deaths, 846 new cases UK.

31st: The highest temperature of the summer, 37.8°C recorded at Heathrow Airport making it the third hottest day ever recorded in the UK.

To cope with the heat and the lockdown we invested in a children's 8.5 ft paddling pool. This simple thing gave my daughter and I so much relief, and lots of fun. We even splashed about in it during the night time rainstorms. The letting go and being childish was cathartic. My neighbour thought we had lost the plot.

August

3rd: UK Government launches 'Eat Out to Help Out', a half price meal scheme encouraging the public to get out and spend money in pubs and restaurants.

4th: An explosion in the port at Beirut kills 204 people.

12th: Tenet fever grips the U.K., claiming over 50% of ticket sales in the cinemas that are open.

13th: Study by Imperial College London suggests 3.4 million people in England have had coronavirus, 10 times higher than official figures.

25th: Africa declared free from wild polio.

31st: Covid 2 UK deaths, new cases 1406 UK.

The first time we went to the hairdressers during the pandemic was in late August; it was a big deal, something both my daughter and I had been desperate for. The rules meant we could only go into the salon one at a time, no waiting inside for pending customers. We made a plan. I would go into the salon first. While I had my hair done, my daughter would cover off half our shopping list and then we would swap roles. I came out of the salon with a wonderful head on the outside but a muddled one on the inside, all the masks and one way had got me a bit flustered. Before my daughter was allowed in, she was asked to pass her shopping bags and coat to me. I looked at the shopping list and noticed the only items left to buy were balsamic vinegar, vegan mayo, black mustard seeds and yeast. Easy, all I had to do was cross the road to the health food shop to get them, which I did. I still had time to wander and rather than do so aimlessly I plucked up courage to visit the antiques bizarre. The rules were strict; had to wear a mask, keep two metres apart and the number of people allowed in was limited to ten; there are about twelve rooms and large corridors to walk through and it seemed safe enough. On entry I had to douse my hands in sanitizer; the guy at the door warned me it was greasy and it was. I struggled to sanitize up and keep hold of my purchases, the shopping bags and my daughters coat but managed eventually. I spent a few minutes looking at the paraphernalia; I spotted a colourful china 1930's salt and pepper set in one of the back rooms; I thought to buy it for my daughter as she is a keen cook and lover of vintage kitchen gear. As I bent forward slowly to put my load down and examine the cruet set, the balsamic vinegar slipped through my still very greasy hands. I screamed as the bottle smashed on the tiled floor, splashing its contents over oak furniture, crystal glassware, earthenware jugs and my bare legs. The glass splintered all around me. As I stepped back, some glass that had landed in my slip-on shoes pressed deep into my heel. Now there was blood adding to the mess. My heel was cut quite badly. I panicked. I hobbled to the back of the emporium where the attendant was selling a Victorian table to an older couple, and planned to own up to my blunder. But I saw the exit sign and bolted out. I staggered back to the hairdressing salon with blood and vinegar dripping off my right foot. Local shoppers and tourists looked at me aghast as I hobbled down the high street but I kept my head down. I plonked myself down on the bench outside the hairdressers and sobbed. My daughter and the receptionist came out within a few minutes and helped clean me up. My beige suede shoes were ruined stained a reddish brown. I felt stupid. I can laugh now but what a palaver. £6.50 of good vinegar wasted and a spoilt pair of good sandals. I have not yet had the guts to return to the emporium to apologise; I will one day.

September

2nd: steroids, dexamethasone and hydrocortisone, found to improve survival of critically ill Covid-19 patients.
6th: Police in Hong Kong fire pepper-spray balls at crowds protesting against the Chinese governments' decision

to delay legislative elections in the territory with nearly 300 people arrested.

7th: Wikileaks co-founder Julian Assange appears in the dock at London's Old Bailey as his fight against extradition to the US resumes.

9th: UK bans gatherings of more than 6 people over fears about a second wave.

10th: Covid 14 deaths, 2919 new cases UK.

16th: President Trump claims that coronavirus will just 'go away' due to 'herd mentality'.

24th: Study finds that coronavirus is continuing to mutate.

30th: Covid 71 deaths, 7108 new cases UK.

As the weeks turned into months and the summer faded into autumn, we were becoming accustomed to the temporary hold the pandemic had placed on our lives. September is my favourite month, still warm, but not burning sunshine, warm evenings to still sit outdoors and gentle winds blowing the conkers off the trees. I decided to venture into Wales to see my brother; crossing the border into a country with its own rules and regulations for Covid-19. I ventured into my homeland just as the Welsh Government locked down Caerphilly. My route to my brothers isolated off-grid sheep farmer's bwthyn (cottage) avoided travelling near Caerphilly, but I was nevertheless nervous of the rise in the infection rate in Wales at the time. I had visions of me being stranded in mid-Wales for weeks, so I packed plenty of bras and pants just in case. It was great to be tucked away from the world, on top of the hills overlooking the Brecon Beacons; greens, browns and tans dusting the summits, a blue sky touching the defined ridges, silhouetting the woodlands. I woke up my first morning alive and ready to go. I had offered to help my brother and his wife with any jobs; they were slowly renovating what had been a rundown dwelling and there was still much to do. I wanted to earn my keep and forget the world outside; some hard labour would do me good. Or so I thought.

The first job was, according to my brother, straight-forward. We were to go and fetch his 4x4 from the local garage. The car had been there for nearly a month for repairs as his wife did not drive and there was no rush as they had other vehicles. Straightforward? Drive ten miles down the upper Tywi valley, pick the 4x4 from Llandovery and back to the wilderness. However, the track up to my brothers' bwthyn is really a rut lane for the quad bikes the sheep farmers use. It is a treacherous trail to drive and only vehicles built for off-road driving can manage the terrain. The rutted lane shoots off from what is not in any way a main road, but more of a rough single track leading to civilisation at one end and nature reserves and private wood-land at the other. As we bump down to the main road, I expect my brother to turn right so we can pick up my car which is safely parked in the church carpark. I assume we will use my car to do the errand. But no, as we turn left my brother explains his plan; I can drive the VW 4X4 we are currently travelling in back home from the garage. Shit. I feel sick. I feel the panic rise in my throat; my chest pumps, my mouth is dry; I can't think. I want to run away. I'm getting scared. I'm panicking. Panicking. Panicking.

I am an experienced driver. I completed an advanced driver course (not long after passing my driving test) when I was first working as a sales rep in the South Wales valleys. The company I was working for at the time put all the field sales team through the course. I did pass with the highest score of the lot as I was the most cautious driver. And as a successful rep I had also been lucky to win a bonus for high sales with the prize of a track day, with the chance to drive all manner of vehicles from rally cars, F4 racing cars to jalopy wagons. All under the supervision of experienced racing drivers, I learnt about speed and spatial awareness. Just to say, I am not a speed queen, and it took me ages to get the hang of driving an F4. I hopped and spluttered around the track most of the time, as my colleagues joked about for weeks after the event.

I'm happy driving most cars but draw the line at vans and 4x4s: they are so big and often times I cannot reach the pedals or see clearly over the bonnet. When I drive large vehicles, I feel as if I am actually, physically using my own body to propel the machine forward, and so as a little person, I don't do big cars.

Back to Wales in the September of 2020; my brother and I on the way to pick up his 4x4. My panic begins to bubble up. Unaware of my anxiety my brother is talking about how the VW works. I can't take it all in but I get the gist that there is an automatic and off-road option. I breathe slowly, I watch as my brother navigates the narrow road. I make mental notes about the route, the narrow bends, the overgrown hedges, the streams crossing the single-track low dips, the badly parked cars, the passing places and farmyard entrances. I clock all this for the journey back. We arrive at the garage, my brother parks up and vacates the driving seat. I climb into the driver's side of the VW and I mean climb because it's bloody high up and I am not able to manage a ladylike slide over. I fiddle with the gears and manage to inch the VW forward and back. Great start, I can at least move the car. However, I end up blocking the entrance to the garage. Life is slower in Mid-Wales (and dare I say, the standard of driving poorer in these rural communities) and no one is bothered as I take a full five minutes to edge the truck out of the way. Most of the waiting people have their car windows down and are chatting happily to each other whilst mildly wondering what this red-headed woman is doing in what they know to be my brothers' vehicle.

Once we head off for the return journey, I realise I can see easily in the VW, and using the automatic gear function works well for me; all I have to do is follow the path of my brother. I am convinced the 4x4 he's driving is bigger than the VW I am in and I reason I am safe to do what he does in terms of passing and manoeuvring the traffic. The ten miles from the local market town to the bottom of his track are hard work; I am concentrating; I am gripping the wheel; I have clenched teeth; I am focused on the road, anticipating the landmarks and danger spots as best I can. I safely pass caravans, army trucks, motorbikes, food delivery vans, tractors, and cyclists. I tell myself I can do this. I am doing this. I am okay. I am safe. We get to the bottom of the track for the bwthyn and I know I cannot drive much more. I cannot manage to take the 4x4 the last mile up to the cottage. I cannot navigate the deep crevices, the fallen trees, the slippery slate slope, and the hard steep drop off the passenger side. This is a road for experts only; brave and experienced experts. I am not that person, PTSD or not. My brother obviously thinks otherwise. The panic returns and this time the pain in my chest hurts; I am sweating so much my hands and the small of my back are wet with perspiration. I am shaking, my legs have turned to jelly. I want to cry. I am frozen with fear. My brother shouts over to keep the vehicle moving at a steady pace; he will open the gates. I just have to drive in off-road mode and the 4x4 will do the rest. I go to speak, to say no, but no words come out. My tongue is stuck to the roof of my mouth. My bother moves off and I sit there for a while, immobilised with terror. Then my brother is shouting back as he does the first gate 'you can do this sis, you really can'. My brother trusts me and that kicks me out of my fear gear. I start deep breathing and reciting the days of the week in Welsh. I am gripping the wheel tightly; I am leaning forward to will the car to safety. I do not look to the left, to the harsh slopping drop into a ravine in the woods, to the precipice inches away from the passenger side wheels. I recite the months of the year in Welsh. I breathe. I focus. I think of nothing but following my brother's tracks. I will do this. I will. I must. I can. As the bwthyn comes into view I start to relax; I am thinking to celebrate with a G&T rather than a cuppa. I deserve and need the gin. Within metres of the front yard, I hear a loud bang and the 4x4 lunges to the left. I hit a mossy bank. There has been a blowout on the front passenger side tyre. Had that happened minutes before I would have been a goner; the 4x4 would have slipped down the valley sides and I would have hit a tree or two for sure. I would have had no control over the truck and stood little chance of coming out with a serious injury. The tyres on the VW were due for a replacement hence my brother's keenness to get his second vehicle, but the timing was luck (good or bad luck is the question). I jumped out of the truck and nearly collapsed with relief. I was shaking even more than earlier and ended up laughing and crying hysterically. It had been an exhausting afternoon, but I was strengthened by my determination to try, and trust. To trust myself, and my brother!

That night over a few G&Ts I explained the details of the saga to my brother; I told him a little bit more about how PTSD was impacting me. He was silent for a while (not often seen), apologised for not realising and helped me recognise the brave Me was fighting back. He also pointed out that I was mistaken about the size differences between the 4x4s, they were both similar sizes. Thankfully my poor perception had worked in my favour, giving me a false confidence. The techniques I had learnt during therapy had worked, albeit in extreme circumstances. I knew I had overcome my fear successfully and that felt good. I was not a prisoner to it. I had been so, so scared, and that was reasonable but I had managed it, I had limited its negative impact. I had not let the fear overwhelm me. This was a breakthrough.

By the time I left my brothers a few days later I was mentally and physically exhausted, but in a good way. It was as if I'd been to an army boot camp or on an adventure holiday. Over the days I had lifted slate tiles and removed the crusted lime from the backs using a power tool; I had helped fell ash trees and stack the logs into neat piles for the winter. I even managed to stay upright as their four Leonberger dogs bounced about me on walks around Llyn Brianne dam, and fought for morning cuddles from the visitor. I'd watched red kites, starlings, coal tits, kestrels, sparrow hawks, a tawny owl and whinchats fly freely in the fresh air as if I had nothing to do but take pleasure from seeing them. I was able to switch off and just be me. Me with still a little bit of PTSD.

October

1st: COVID-19 restrictions are simplified in England into a three-tier system following confusion over local rules.
9th: The 22-year-old Manchester United and England footballer Marcus Rashford given an MBE for his

campaign to force the Prime Minister to support free meals for school children during the pandemic.

19th: University of Edinburgh palaeontologists identify the remains of 71-75-million-year tyrannosaurs that hadn't broken free from their shells; revealing that baby tyrannosaurs were about the size of a Chihuahua, with an extra-long tail.

20th: UK try the first coronavirus 'challenge trials', infecting young people with the virus to speed up vaccine development.

23rd: The coronavirus fatality rate in England increases for the first time since the peak back in April.

31st October: 326 deaths, 21,915 new cases UK. James Bond actor Sir Sean Connery dies, age 90, peacefully in his sleep.

By the autumn of 2020 we were still facing many restrictions due to the Covid pandemic and the national and local situations were disconcerting, depressing and a tad boring. The previous autumn's news had been boring with Brexit, but not as depressing or disconcerting as the pandemic. Covid-19 was too close to home. It was impacting on all our lives on a daily basis and there seemed to be no end in sight. This uncertainty was not helping me deal with the PTSD as well as I might have done had there been no pandemic. My anxiety and fear seemed to be in step with the rises in the infection rate, hospital admissions and death rates. My anxiety would map well with the UK government Covid-19 new cases data, 1st August 771, 1st September 1,295, 1st October 6,914, 4th October 22,961. The death rate was rising too. As of 15th October, 57,690 people in the UK had died with Covid-19 stated on their death certificate.

I had to work bloody hard to stop myself worrying unduly about my children. I had to work unbelievably hard to stop the dread. The dread that one day they would get Covid-19 and either die or suffer long Covid. This dread and fear of death was draining and during the autumn months I consciously had to slow down. I had to stock up my energy, my emotional reserves. I had been busy in the weeks leading into the autumn filling the cupboard and freezer, making tomato chutney, quince jelly, blackberry jam, ratatouille, and carrot soup. I had been walking and gardening and writing this story. There had been the death of my father-in-law and we'd been back to Wales for the funeral. My son had started University and my daughter and I had been to visit him in his new flat. The thing I had learnt in the last year was to listen to my body. My IBS and Lichen Planus were playing up. I knew this was a signal to slow down and recharge and to deal with my distress. I could not let the fear creep back and overwhelm me. I had the skills to deal with my dread. It was as if I was playing snakes and ladders. I had been making great progress over the summer moving up the emotional ladders but now I was slipping down the Covid snakes. I was not going to leave things to chance. My life was not a game. I spent a lot of time remembering how far I had come with getting unstuck from the PTSD. I let my daughter do most of the driving at this time and that was wonderful. When I got stuck my friends and neighbours helped with some of the heavy things that needed doing in the garden and around the house. I was not too proud to accept the help. I recognised we were in this for the long run and so best to accept my limitations. I made sure I got the flu jab as soon as it became available and we all took care to minimise our exposure risk. Covid-19 and my PTSD were a match made in hell.

November

Things are getting worse, not better.

Approx. 450 people a day are dying from Covid with well over 20,000 new cases a day. The numbers start to mean nothing—they are too big and scary to grapple with. The total number of people who are dying in the UK is now more than other European countries. Where are we going wrong?

1st: England win the Six Nations rugby championship, with Wales coming 5th.

2nd: Global Covid death toll passes 1.2 million.

5th: Remember, remember the 5th of November, the UK government imposes a 2nd lockdown in response to a rise in Covid cases. The lockdown is to run for a month to 2nd December.

9th: Pfizer announces that its Covid-19 vaccine is 90% effective.

22nd: Lab-confirmed coronavirus cases pass 1.5 million in the UK.

25th: World soccer player Diego Armando Maradona dies, and Argentina mourns the loss of 'El Dios' (The God).

30th: Final results show the Moderna vaccine to be 94% effective and nobody who was given the vaccine in test trials developed severe disease.

My routine, my To-do and Not To-do lists help me cope. I am bored with the pandemic but not bored with life or living. I am managing to stay on top of my anxiety and the depressive symptoms of the PTSD are negligible. I remain scared, but then who's not at this time. Me and my family are zealous about the restrictions as this is the only way we can stay safe until we get a Covid vaccine. I am not sure if the forced isolation is doing me good or not; I am making the most of WhatsApp and Zoom, calling friends all over the world and even taking part in theatre type events. I have reason to despair beyond Covid and PTSD. The news is depressing. If it's not Covid, it's some dictator ruining the show, spoiling democratic processes or trying to shut good citizens up or lock opponents away. I try to focus on what I can do to make the world a better place. I focus on the changes I can make; I consider how to effectively rid our shopping of single use plastic and I experiment with seasonal vegetable recipes. I bore my friends with pictures of my vegan food, not a meal goes past without a 'snap and share'.

December

2nd: Pfizer/BioNTech Covid vaccine judged safe for use in UK.

4th: WHO warns against complacency generated by the creation of successful vaccines, warning that the pandemic still has a long way to go.

10th: Dame Barber Windsor dies age 83 after suffering with Alzheimer's Disease.

12th: David Cornwell, known as John le Carre, author and spy, dies aged 89.

14th: WHO declares that Santa Claus is immune to coronavirus.

15th: Christmas is coming. Number of new daily cases in the UK is hovering around 25,000 with over 400 people dying each day. Things are not going in the right direction.

19th: The total number of coronavirus cases globally passes 75 million.

20th: A new Covid variant in the UK is considered, by government advisers, to be 70% more transmittable than other variants.

24th: The European Commission and the UK reach an agreement on the terms of future cooperation in light of Brexit. Study suggests that England could face more Covid-19 deaths in the next six months than in the whole of 2020 unless restrictions are increased.

25th: The only day over the Christmas period that most of the UK is allowed to celebrate with members of their household and/or support bubbles. No-one is allowed to travel to see family and friends in other parts of the UK.

26th: Storm Bella brings heavy rain and strong winds to parts of the UK with a wind gust of 106 mph recorded on the Isle of Wight, and the highest gust recorded in 2020.

28th: UK reports over 40,000 cases in 24 hours for the first time since the start of the pandemic.

30th: The AstaZeneca Covid-19 vaccine is approved for use in adults in the UK.

31st: Brexit transition period ends and the UK leaves the EU for good.

We had a relaxing family Christmas. There were no difficult decisions to make about who should come; my son came home from university to be with my daughter and I. The most difficult thing was deciding whether to do an all-vegan Christmas dinner or cater for those pining for a traditional turkey feast. We managed to keep everybody happy.

Everything I'd learnt, and was still learning, proved to be a blessing in disguise. Dealing with 'distress-intolerance' was the theme of our family discussions. Sharing the past years' experiences with my troops enabled them to manage their own fears, anxieties and frustrations. We were all shit scared. We were all struggling to see the light at the end of the Covid tunnel. We all felt imprisoned and powerless by Covid-19. Having each other to talk with was like getting under a cosy duvet when the night is cold and stormy outside.

January 2021

Happy New Year?

1st: UK leaves the EU Single Market and Customs Union, and all EU policies and international agreements. The free movement of persons, goods, services and capital between the UK and the EU ends.

3rd: UK death toll passes 75,000.

4th: England enters third national lockdown. UK becomes the first country to administer the Oxford-Astra-Zeneca vaccine.

5th: GCSEs and A-Level examinations cancelled in the UK for 2020/21 as the UK's Chief Medical Officer, Chris Whitty announces that 1 in 50 people in the UK has coronavirus.

13th: The UK passes 100,000 coronavirus deaths (just like the Christmas Eve warning).

14th: Archaeologists discover the world's oldest known animal cave painting in Indonesia, a wild pig, drawn 45,500 years ago.

15th: The NHS is on its knees; hospital admissions are reaching 4000 a day by the middle of the month.

20th: 1820 people die of Covid in one day. The total numbers of people who have died to date are, over 93K for the UK, and 2.06M globally. Joe Biden is peacefully inaugurated as the 46th president of the United States and Kamala Harris becomes the first female, first Black, first South Asian US Vice President-Elect.

23rd: One year since Wuhan entered lockdown, confining its 11 million citizens to their homes.

Later in the spring......

March

23rd: On the UK's national day of reflection I have my first Covid vaccination, a year to the day of lockdown in England.

27th: Wales beat France to win the 2021 Six Nations rugby tournament.

I am working to finish my mansion; writing this book has been cathartic. I feel a glimmer of hope (I 'do' do hope now) as the Covid-19 vaccines are approved and rolled out in the UK. I still feel like my glue is not dry but I don't feel so fragile that a light wind would blow me over, or pull me apart; I think I could withstand a strong breeze but nothing like a gale or storm yet.

Space

The pandemic forced me to rethink many things. Things I had taken for granted. Things I did not even think needed thinking about, that had not been of consideration before. The greatest of these things was Space. Never before had I realised how sanity sustaining space was. Physical, mental and financial space were becoming critical differentiators of the pandemic. I thanked the stars for the space I had. My space. I wasn't going to let Covid steal or crowd my space. My space. I was going to protect my mental space; I had been working on that for months now to tackle my PTSD. I was not going to let a bloody virus take my mental space. I was fortunate to have physical and financial space to endure the pandemic. I couldn't imagine how I would have fared without either. I watched the news and saw the suffering and problems that lack of space was creating for many people; much of it leading to a mental unhealth pandemic.

Space is a necessity, not a luxury. Looking at Maslow's hierarchy of needs, I consider that space should fall into the first block of the pyramid, as one of our physiological needs. The biological requirements for human survival, include air, food, drink, clothing, warmth, chances for reproduction, sleep and shelter. Shelter is much more than a roof over our heads, the safe space in which we live; it is about having physical and mental freedom and privacy to do all the other things in the Maslow's first block.

Decent Physical, Financial and Mental Space = Good Mental Wellbeing

Room to
work
play
teach
learn
relax

Room to
sleep
cook
eat
binge watch the telly
Zoom

Room to
dance
think
shield
keep fit
socialise

Room to be

Staying Connected

Friendship helped pull me from the PTSD pit. Without my friends I would not have endured the pain of PTSD. They listened, they cared, they cajoled, they advised, they laughed and cried with me. Above all though it was their honesty that held me up. They would not let me fall. Despite Covid I manage to stay well connected to my friends, all courtesy in the main from Zoom and WhatsApp. I have one friend in the USA who initially was very frustrated with my not doing mainstream social media; she wanted to keep me abreast of all her adventures and with the time difference it was not easy to talk on the phone. But I will give credit to her that she became great at directly sending me her pictures via WhatsApp. In return, I sent her pictures of my vegetable growing, my vegan dishes, my crocheted blankets and short videos of my walks or escapades with my daughter in our kiddie paddling pool. I found this way of communicating such fun. When I felt well and was in a good place, I would reach out over WhatsApp to my friends across the world and share my thoughts and creations with them. During the pandemic this staying connected was like a shot of caffeine, picking me up, giving some oomph, stopping any moping or self-pity. As the saying goes, 'a problem shared is a problem halved'. This went both ways as I tried to be a good listening friend back; 'good things come to those that give back' as the saying goes.

On Friendship

And a youth said, Speak to us of Friendship.
And he answered, saying:
Your friend is your needs answered.
He is your field which you sow with love and reap with thanksgiving.
And he is your board and your fireside.
For you come to him with your hunger, and you seek him for peace.

When your friend speaks his mind you fear not the "nay" in your own mind, nor do you withhold the "ay."
And when he is silent your heart ceases not to listen to his heart;
For without words, in friendship, all thoughts, all desires, all expectations are born and shared, with joy that is unacclaimed.
When you part from your friend, you grieve not;

For that which you love most in him may be clearer in
his absence, as the mountain to the climber is clearer
from the plain.
And let there be no purpose in friendship save the
deepening of the spirit.
For love that seeks aught but the disclosure of its own
mystery us not love but a net cast forth: and only the
unprofitable is caught.

And let your best be for your friend.
If he must know the ebb of your tide, let him know its
flood also.
For what is your friend that you should seek him with
hours to kill?
Seek him always with hours to live.
For it is his to fill your need but not your emptiness.
And in the sweetness of friendship let there be laughter,
and sharing of pleasures.
For in the dew of little things the heart finds its morning
and is refreshed.

From Kahlil Gibran, *The Prophet* (Knopf, 1923)

The Internet and Digital Stuff

Whilst in the pit of fear and struggling with the worst of PTSD, I couldn't sit at the PC. It was the last place I wanted to be, in front of a screen. I didn't consult the internet for self-help. I couldn't. I didn't want to sit in front of a monitor: I'd have been staring at a blur of words. Concentrating was hard when things were bad. But coming to the end of my scribbles I came across a number of online resources I wish I'd been aware of at the time I was most lost. I'm not sure how much they would have changed things for me, but I know moving forward they will be useful as I continue my journey with PTSD.

I will admit I have serious reservations about looking up health information on the internet. I would advise only going to an official charity or medical website, or use resources recommended by professionals. I would also warn against using the web to diagnose a condition like PTSD; I know many people that as soon as they see a list of symptoms, worry they have the condition. That said PTSD is well represented on the internet and there are some really good and informative websites, for instance MIND UK has a great list of links to other websites covering specific aspects of trauma and victim support for child abuse, road accidents and torture.

PTSD UK

Charity set up in 2015 by a lady who experienced PTSD; her mission is to provide support and information for anyone experiencing PTSD in the UK. The charity campaigns to improve services, raise awareness and promote understanding of the condition and the treatments available in the UK. The information on the site is easy to digest, written with the understanding of a sufferer and very practical.

https://www.ptsduk.org/

HelpGuide

HelpGuide helps you help yourself. It is a small independent non-profit organisation that runs one of the world's top 10 mental health websites. Over 50 million people from all around the world have been able to access free trustworthy content which has empowered them to improve their mental health by making relevant changes. The website covers a wide range of mental health disorders, with useful tips to deal with trauma and PTSD.

HelpGuide.org

UK NHS Resources

The NHS website, Every Mind Matters has expert advice and practical tips to help you look after your mental health and wellbeing. There is simple quiz that you can complete online to get some straightforward advice.

https://www.nhs.uk/oneyou/every-mind-matters/

The information on self-help for PTSD on Scotland's Service Directory NHS inform may be helpful for people waiting to get professional help. This guide does explain how to use grounding.

https://www.nhsinform.scot/illnesses-and-conditions/mental-health/mental-health-self-help-guides/ptsd-and-cptsd-self-help-guide

The UK NHS website suggest people see a GP if they are still having problems four weeks after a traumatic experience, or if symptoms are particularly troublesome.

https://www.nhs.uk/conditions/post-traumatic-stress-disorder-ptsd/

MIND

This is an established charity and offers support across the mental health spectrum. There is a lot of good, detailed information on the site about PTSD. The organisation has a strong community focus with 125 local UK network groups and staff supporting 91 GP surgeries.

https://www.mind.org.uk/

SHOUT

Shout is a 24/7 UK crisis text service available for people in need of immediate mental health support. Shout was launched in May 2019, and is part of Mental Health innovations (MHI), which was founded in November

2017. MHI was set up following the success of The Royal Foundation's 'Heads Together' campaign, which identified that digital platforms and tools do help individuals struggling with their mental health.

https://www.giveusashout.org/

Mental Health UK

Mental Health UK supports people affected by mental health problems including friends, family and carers. Working across the UK, they work to improve understanding and provide vital care with advice (including financial), information, support groups and digital platforms. PTSD is well covered on the website with a very useful page on other useful sources and contacts.

https://mentalhealth-uk.org/

Oxford Mindfulness Centre

The Oxford Mindfulness Centre's (OMC) mission is to reduce suffering, promote resilience and realise human potential across the lifespan through mindfulness. They have a batch of twelve informal, free podcasts covering Mindfulness. I found these useful and easy to access and listen to.

https://www.oxfordmindfulness.org/learn-mindfulness/online-sessions-podcasts/

PTSD: National Centre for PTSD

This is a site based in the USA and aimed at helping veterans and their families. This site has a good publications database covering the research into PTSD. The site is available in Spanish too.

https://www.ptsd.va.gov/

Tech & Apps

One of the areas I struggle with, despite my progress with managing anxiety, is the fear my children will die in a car accident. I know I have to get this into perspective. The lockdown was a bit of relief to me as this meant my troops were not going out and about. But once the restrictions were lifted, I had to face the fact that they were both going to be driving on a regular basis. I could not live with high levels of anxiety just because life was getting back to normal. It was not fair on them or good for me. So, my daughter introduced me to an App that allows sharing of journeys when travelling and this proved a successful way to dramatically reduce my anxiety. The fact that I could almost see how the journey was going in real time, in that the car was progressing along the right route, took away all the unreasonable worry and my feeling became just those of mild concern that they arrived at their destination safely. I could not believe how something so simple could work; it was the reassurance and the taking away of the uncertainty that the App helped with. Thumbs up to technology.

I found managing restless twitchy hyper states difficult and when combined with lack of concentration, I could not switch off. It seemed impossible to get out of the rut. Walking helped for a while but then I would march myself into exhaustion. Once again, my daughter had another solution. Podcasts. The range of topics was mind blowing; there was so much to delve into, serious, fun, highbrow, witty, political, satirical, historical, current affairs, people, and places. At the touch of a button

I lost myself in the voices of the narrator, journalist or story teller; I switched off. Jittery Me appeased; no more ants in pants, no more cat on hot bricks, no more hee-bie-jeebies.

No Harm Meant

Qualifying but not apologising per se for any offence in my scribbles, no harm meant. I've no doubt written some things in a way that offends others. During the development of this book, I tried to remove any hurtful or judgemental thoughts of mine. Just to be clear, I mean no disrespect to:

- Religious communities
- Pessimists
- Introverts
- Employers
- Famous people
- My school music teacher
- The Welsh (especially car drivers)
- Short people
- Ginger haired folk
- The NHS
- Therapists
- Female gas and electric meter readers
- People who do Social Media
- The elderly
- Authors of self-help books
- People with mental illness

Measures of Success

At the beginning of my recovery, I considered that getting back to work should be my ultimate aim. If I could get back into the groove, withstand the hustle and bustle, cope with stresses and strains of a leadership role I would be doing well. By late spring of 2020 I came to see this was a narrow and unhelpful way to look at the success, or not, of my therapy. Being an avid list maker, I made a list of the small, day to day, practical things that would be a sign I was on the road to recovery, that things were going in the right direction and I was making progress. I gave the items on my list a scale and at the end of every week I would rate the items. By 2021, despite the Covid pandemic, I was making good progress in some areas; the flashbacks and bad language were no more; the bad dreams came less often and although worried about the virus I was less crippled by the anxiety. This system helped me track my progress visually and on bad days I could draw strength from small gains. At one end of the scale was 0% i.e., still have the issue at a crippling level; 50% still have the issue but not disabling me; 100% problem gone.

My list was simple:

Flashbacks
Nightmares
Screaming readily
Hyper twitchy, can't settle to anything, overdoing cleaning
Bad language/blunt talk
Passive aggressive or clipped communications
Confident driving/timely crossing of the road
Dread of my kids dying
Black days/deep despair/crippling sadness/guilt ridden
Avoiding people/not wanting to go out
Solving problems that are not mine/OTT planning

As a write, I can report that most of the time my dial is set on the right side of the 50%, an issue but not disabling me. I am completely free of the flashbacks and have no problems driving and crossing the road, 100% gone, nightmares and screaming readily are approaching resolution at 95%. I think that is good progress for eighteen months of treatment, with a pandemic to boot.

Measuring success would usually be part of any follow up of medical care. During follow up, experience teams will formally assess your progress with therapy and if prescribed, medication. These formal assessments are important. During the seven months of my privately funded therapy a track was kept on my progress with informal discussion and scoring on the PTSD scale IES-R. It is worth mentioning for those who take alternative routes to care, make sure your medical records reflect the care you receive. Make sure your day-to-day doctor has the details of your diagnosis and therapy. This is particularly important for mental health as general practitioners are not often well placed to provide ongoing specialist support and monitoring for PTSD, especially if you have not gone via the NHS (this applies to the UK, but in other countries the issue is not dissimilar when care is provided in different settings).

Half Way Down the Mountain

As I write this part of my story, It's over two years on from when I first noticed the disabling symptoms of PTSD and I am in a very different place. I'm amazed how much better I know myself; I am happy to be alive. I am not confused or overwhelmed by unfamiliar emotions. I have learnt to tolerate distress. However, learning to do something when you are stressed or sick is bloody hard work; it is a fine line to catching the problem in time to cope. How do we learn to be ready to cope with distress? How do we learn to shovel the shit that comes our way? We need a bank of skills, experience and a mind set to deal positively with trouble; how do we get that? How do we build resilience?

I remember when my children were growing up, I taught them to willingly swallow tablets and nasty tasting medicine well before they hit 18 months. In fact, my son had to take horrid tasting liquid salbutamol for his asthma as a baby and so he was well trained; By two years old I was teaching him to use asthma inhalers. All this training was a godsend when they were sick as we had no crying, or pursed lips or tantrums over taking essential medication. There was no need for flying 5 ml plastic spoons, squirting medication through a syringe, bribery or trickery. When we play dangerous sports, we protect ourselves with padding or helmets; we do this because there are risks, there is the potential to get hurt; so, we protect ourselves, we anticipate and we prepare.

Talking is good padding. I talked to my children proactively about life, death, disease, loss, pain, disability, suffering, harm, prejudice, and bullying as they grew up. I did so because from an early age we saw much suffering in the hospital beds around us when my children were sick. We were aware of the children and young adults that did not make it out of hospital. We could not ignore the facts and the heavy pain of the families involved, it seemed right to acknowledge this at the time. You don't have to be profound or have answers, it helped us to just talk and give my children the chance to ask questions. I learnt one thing though, you do have to be honest and use language that makes sense (age appropriate). If you don't, you store trouble for the future. I believe it was this approach that enabled my children to help me deal with PTSD. Talking honestly takes courage.

We are all different; we face different traumas; when shit hits the fan, we are at different starting points with our skills and resilience; we have access to different resources and support networks. From reading about mental health and certainly from my experience, there is no one perfect cure, no one size fits all; it's more of a pick and mix. Work with what you've got, make the most of that, and then plug the gap with what is missing. But above all don't give up, keep talking or communicating through the channels that work for you. Keep the padding on.

When learning to ride a bike as children we expect to fall off a few times once the stabilisers are removed. I may be a controlling person and in the worst days of my PTSD I was anticipating all sorts of trouble: I have come to realise that it is no bad thing to pre-empt things that could knock us off our bike. I believe preparing and protecting yourself is important to building resilience. Instead of asking 'why me?', I say 'why not me?' Shit's going to happen to someone, but I'm going to make dam sure I prevent (prevention better than cure adage) as much coming my way as I can; but if it does, I have the shovel ready.

I said at the beginning of this story that my journey out of PTSD was hard work, along a path untrodden. It has been a bumpy ride but one that has taught me to be gracious, patient and kind to myself and others. I have learnt to think differently about and respond to the negative things that happen; I have learnt to trust others; I have made new friends along the way; and I recognise and understand other peoples' pain so much better. You can stop trauma sticking to you, sucking the life out of you. You really can. It is worth all the effort and tears. I have not forgotten my traumatic experiences, I never will. But I can recall those events without reliving the horror. I can think of the bad times without a rush of dread. I am not plagued by flashbacks and nightmares. I am not stuck in the past. I am very much in the present experiencing all its challenges (mainly Covid and sorting out an amicable divorce). I have the support of my children and friends and an acute awareness that I have been fortunate. I got help before my PTSD strangled me for ever. I look forward to the future with cautious optimism. And for me that is progress. I am being realistic about life moving forward as opposed to swinging between dreading things and being unbearably positive. I am not going to fear negative shit from now on. I am going to experience things as they come, good or bad, happy or sad. I am going to feel my way through life from now on. Really feel. So much better for my mental wellbeing don't you think?

It was the love and support of my family and friends that made my journey with PTSD bearable. Talking about my pain was my way out of PTSD. So, where do I go from here? I've travelled with PTSD for a very long time. I've not yet dropped my burdensome passenger off, but it's nearly time for that. I am close to my final, safe, destination. Since starting to scribble in early 2020, I've left my job, initiated a divorce from my husband, packed my youngest off to University, had a rewarding time living in lockdown with my daughter, gone vegan, and learnt to adapt to a world with Covid-19. I have no idea what the future holds for me, but I know I do have a future without PTSD. I've evolved and I have a life to live. My life. PTSD free.

> "But that is the beginning of a new story—the story of the gradual renewal of a man, the story of his gradual regeneration, of his passing from one world into another, of his initiation into a new unknown life. That might be the subject of a new story, but our present story is ended."

Crime and Punishment, Fyodor Dostoyevsky,
The Russian Messenger. Translated by Constance Garnett
London: Heinemann (1914)

Facts About PTSD—Techy Stuff at the Back

Up to this point I have tried to impart limited technical information through my story. However, there are some facts about PTSD that I have found helpful. Facts that along the way have enabled me to understand why, and accept that, my PTSD was disabling me. I have filtered some of this information and provide some places that provide credible intel for the layman.

Definitions

PTSD is a common, serious, and complex mental disorder that occurs following exposure to traumatic events. It is characterised by intrusive thoughts and reexperiencing the trauma through flashback-like dissociative reactions, efforts to avoid trauma-related thoughts, feelings, places, or people, persistent negative cognition and mood, and hyperarousal, such as anxiety, sleep difficulties, and irritability. Failed recovery from PTSD can have long-term harmful effects on an individual's social function, family life, occupational responsibilities and personal health. PTSD can be triggered by traumatic events such as real or threatened death, severe injury or sexual assault. It is essentially a memory filing error caused by the traumatic event.

Facts

- Two million people in the UK are affected by PTSD but only 1 in 4 get treatment.
- Statistics show that about 2 in 3 people with PTSD eventually get better without treatment, although the improvement may take several months.
- Most people will experience a traumatic event at some point in their life, and up to 25 to 33% will develop PTSD, but it's not clear why some people develop the condition and others don't.
- Previous exposure to trauma appears to increase the risk of developing PTSD with subsequent traumatic events.
- Recent research tells us many factors influence the disposition to PTSD, including gender; age at trauma; race; lower education; lower socioeconomic status; being separated, divorced, or widowed; previous trauma; general childhood adversity; personal

and family psychiatric history; childhood abuse; poor social support; and initial severity of reaction to the traumatic event.

- PTSD can be successfully treated, even when it develops many years after a traumatic event.

How does PTSD look in our population (epidemiology)? Many different types of trauma have been found to result in PTSD. These types and the proportion of PTSD cases have recently been identified as:

- Sexual relationship violence—32% (e.g., rape, childhood sexual abuse, intimate partner violence).
- Interpersonal-network traumatic experiences—30% (e.g., unexpected death of a loved one, life-threatening illness of a child, other traumatic event of a loved one).
- Interpersonal violence—12% (e.g., childhood physical abuse or witnessing interpersonal violence, physical assault, or being threatened by violence).
- Exposure to organized violence—3% (e.g., refugee, kidnapped, civilian in war zone).
- Participation in organized violence—11% (e.g., combat exposure, witnessing death/serious injury or discover dead bodies, accidentally or purposefully cause death or serious injury).

- Other life-threatening traumatic events—12% (e.g., life-threatening car crashes, natural disasters, toxic chemical exposure, pandemics).

Not surprisingly PTSD is more common in certain groups of people with research studies showing that PTSD develops in about:

- 1 in 5 firefighters,
- 1 in 3 teenage survivors of car crashes,
- 1 in 2 female rape victims,
- 2 in 3 prisoners of war.

Recent studies (June 2020) have suggested that survivors of COVID-19 are at high risk of developing PTSD and this makes sense considering epidemiological studies had demonstrated a high prevalence of mental health problems among survivors, victim families, medical professionals, and the general public after the epidemics of SARS, MERS, Ebola, flu, HIV/AIDS. This is proving to be the case with reports in the UK of nearly half of intensive care unit (ICU) and anaesthetic staff reporting symptoms consistent with a probable diagnosis of PTSD, severe depression, anxiety, or problem drinking with a small study in Italy showing that 30% of patients hospitalised with Covid-19 went on to suffer PTSD.

You might be asking yourself, 'How do I know if I have PTSD?' Diagnosis and care of mental health conditions can be difficult. Having symptoms of PTSD is different than having PTSD. Symptoms of PTSD can be caused by other mental health conditions, or other health problems. Only a trained professional can confirm a diagnosis of PTSD and determine its severity. However, if you are concerned about your mental health there are a few questions that it might be worth working through to so you can open up a conversation with a GP or mental health professional.

In the past month, have you:

Had nightmares about the trauma or thought about it when you didn't want to?

Tried hard not to think about the trauma, or avoided people or places that remind you of the trauma?

Felt 'on guard', been more jumpy, irritable or had difficulty concentrating?

Felt numb or detached from people, activities, or your surroundings?

Felt guilty or unable to stop blaming yourself or others for the trauma, or any problems following the trauma?

Answering 'yes' to 3 or more of these questions, suggests it would be a good idea to talk to a GP or local mental health team. Answering 'yes' to 3 or more questions does not mean someone has PTSD, only a medical professional can give a diagnosis. If you do anything at all after reading this book, please consider seeking help if you are suffering. I wish I had done so much sooner. I mistakenly thought my PTSD symptoms would go away over time; this was never going to happen, especially in my case as I'd been having symptoms for over a year. Getting treatment for PTSD helps stop it from causing problems in relationships, work, education and life in general. Asking for help was my first step to getting control of my PTSD, and started my path to recovery. Getting treatment for PTSD also helped me deal with my gut and mouth problems that initially I did not realise were linked.

If you've tried treatment before, and you're still having symptoms, I would point out advancements are being made all the time in treatment options for PTSD and it makes sense to try again when ready. We don't have to live with the nightmare of PTSD. For most people, today's treatments can obliterate symptoms altogether.

Others find treatment and support means they are less disabled by PTSD with fewer or less intense symptoms.

Treatments for PTSD, especially non-drug related options are gaining traction and becoming more established as part of mainstream care for maintaining good mental health. I went through CBT and EMDR and also took medication. Addressing PTSD should involve a multi-pronged approach and it needs a personal approach. Treatment needs to work for you, because you do have to work at it. Medication is passive, you just take the tablet, but therapy requires commitment, practice and patience and I found that required stamina (which at times was not something I had in abundance). Therapy requires working with others, including your therapist, GP, family and friends. Don't let people diss your therapy, I had many people laugh at the idea of EMDR working. The therapy treatment options that are available have been tried and tested. I know that most health services across the world today, including the UK NHS, requires evidence that treatments, including therapy, are effective, safe and worth spending the money on.

For some people, the first step in managing PTSD may be watchful waiting, followed by therapeutic options such as individual or group therapy. In the UK NICE guidance (updated in 2018) recommends the use of trauma focused psychological treatments for PTSD in adults, specifically EMDR and trauma focused CBT. Progressive Muscular Relaxation (which has been used for some time to manage anxiety disorders and chronic pain) has recently been proven to help PTSD sufferers, especially with sleep problems. Progressive Muscular Relaxation involves tensing then easing groups of muscles in turn (at 10-20 second intervals), at the same time as taking deep breaths. Accelerated Resolution Therapy (ART) is a relatively new approach and whilst some elements appear similar to EMDR the suggestion from preliminary studies suggest it can help with less session than needed for EMDR. ART has been used to help people overcome common issues, including stress, anxiety, depression, phobias, grief and substance abuse. Because of its focus on helping individuals get past difficult memories, it's thought to be particularly effective for people with PTSD who suffer from recurring images. There are quite a few other psychotherapy and psychosocial interventions used globally for PTSD in adults, and although they are not routinely used in the UK, they may be of interest to some and this resource on the UpToDate website describes dialectical behaviour therapy, coping skills training, interpersonal psychotherapy, psychodynamic psychotherapy, eclectic psychotherapy and service animals. A recent trend in the USA for treating people with PTSD is with the use of Gestalt Therapy. This holistic approach, founded in the 1940s, focuses on unresolved tension, and was recently advocated by two of America's top trauma psychologists as the better option for most trauma survivors.

The guidance for managing PTSD with medication in the UK is very specific and, as with all decisions around any prescribed medication, the decision should be discussed on an individual basis with a doctor. Drug treatment alone is rarely advised to be a suitable option for PTSD, and certainly not one to be considered lightly. Getting to the root of the problem is essential. Antidepressants (such as selective serotonin reuptake inhibitors (SSRI), are considered helpful adjuncts to therapy in treating some adults with PTSD, but in the UK only two medications (paroxetine and sertraline) are licensed specifically for its treatment. Response to drug treatment of PTSD varies greatly, with few robust individual predictors of response available, meaning it is hard to know who will benefit from drug treatment at the outset. Global direction on the role of medication in PTSD highlights the therapeutic goals as a decrease in intrusive thoughts and images, phobic avoidance, pathological hyperarousal, hypervigilance, irritability and anger, and depression. Drug therapies have generally been effective in decreasing hyperarousal and mood (irritability, anger, depression) symptoms, but somewhat less effective for the symptoms of re-experiencing, emotional numbing, and behavioural avoidance.

Family and friends can help people who have been diagnosed with PTSD by:

- Looking out for changes in mood, especially anger and irritability.
- Keeping a look out for changes in behaviour, including taking time off from work, avoiding specific situations and showing more risky behaviours.
- Being ready to listen.
- Asking general questions, but no judging or telling them what to do.
- Giving the person time to talk and not interrupting them.
- Being sensitive to the phases of recovery and make time to check in with the person on an ongoing basis, not just when they are struggling. Ask 'you ok?' twice.
- Encouraging them to seek additional help if the PTSD seems to be disabling or overwhelming and if they show suicidal thoughts.

The ongoing research into PTSD is providing more clues as to why it happens; and in 2020 scientists in the USA appeared to have discovered how fear forms in the brain of mice, offering hope that one day we may be able to help PTSD sufferers switch off traumatic memories before they take too much of a hold.

Before I Go

I finished working on my story in the spring of 2021 with the intention of publishing that year. In preparation for this I turned my attention from the writing to the cover design, the book title, and the choice of a pseudonym. It was here I hit my greatest frustrations. I drove my friends and family nuts with endless suggestions for book titles and a plethora of potential pen names. It is no exaggeration to say that I came up with eighty-six potential book titles and 23 pen names. This story could easily have been called, 'Keeping it together', 'Broad Shoulders' or 'Brain to Mouth'. 'Dandelions and daisies' was a favourite of mine but a friends thought that sounded like a gardening or poetry book. 'Keeping the lid on PTSD' won a few votes as did 'PTSD On The Table', 'About To Snap', 'Stepping Back From The Edge', 'Putting PTSD To Bed', 'Rewiring: Dealing with Traumatic Memories', and 'Unprocessed'. Those that knew me best encouraged me to stick to my original choice and I do hope that others can see the humour and resilient intent of 'Teeth, Hair and Tits'. My thought process and research for a pseudonym was rigorous and it was fun to think how I could reinvent myself. The top runners for a pen name included

Opal Oak, Morgan Cale, Nia Dalloway. Leyla Larne and Elif Ribbon. In the end I realised being me was time consuming enough and at the end of the day it did not seem right to hide the real person in a personal story.

I will admit I questioned if I was doing the right thing by putting my experiences in the public domain. I worried about the impact of sharing such raw emotions on my family. I watched the news tells us we were facing a mental health crisis on account of the Covid-19 pandemic with NHS staff and experts speaking widely and knowledgeable about PTSD. I was not sure my 'insight' and 'journey' (trendy words at the time) were relevant. As the year moved on things at home needed my attention and thus, I decided to put things with the book on hold for a while.

The year moved on, in the April of 2021 Prince Phillip died at the grand age of ninety-nine; in the May we saw the beginnings of the Delta variant of Covid; in the June I celebrated being sixty by climbing Snowdon with my kids; July saw Covid restrictions lift across the UK. The Tokyo Olympics took place late July/early August with the UK coming 4th with 65 medals; mid-August we witnessed the Taliban take Kabul, bringing misery and hardship to the people of Afghanistan; billionaire Elon Musk launched a spaceflight with the first-ever all-civilian crew in September; in October the International Consortium of Investigative Journalists released the Pandora Papers, exposing how some of the most powerful people in the world including more than 330 politicians from 90 countries use secret offshore companies to hide their wealth whilst the Global COVID-19 death toll of recorded cases passes 5 million as the Delta variant continues to surge around the world; at the COP-26 meeting in Glasgow in November countries made what I sincerely hope will not be empty pledges to address climate change; during December Mt Semeru erupts on Java killing 14 people as the first people in the UK are hospitalised with a new variant of Covid-19, with Omicron killing a similar number as the Indonesian volcano. 2021 ends, as does my marriage with my divorce being finalised in December.

A single paragraph does no justice the events of late 2021 both global and personal. But I could not go to publication without letting you know I did get to the place I deserved to be, PTSD free. During the last months of 2021 I experienced a gradual distancing from the disabling symptoms of PTSD. I had a single wish to be totally free of the burden of PTSD. I wanted my life back, even with the limitations of a pandemic. When I felt ready, I knew should try to come off the medication and live my life without dread. I am pleased to say I managed to start 2022 medication and fear free. 'Happy days' as my brother would say.

People do ask me if I am all the stronger for having been through the mill; my answer to that is no. I am not stronger but because I was not weak to begin with. I was always strong, I am a resilient person, I tend to bounce back, I make sure of it. I must explicitly state this, although it may seem arrogant, because PTSD hit me hard even though I was strong, resilient and a born optimist. PTSD disabled me. PTSD crippled my nature. It took away my capacity to cope, it strangled my courage. For a while PTSD redefined what I was able to do, and how I thought. I would have given anything not to have gone through the trauma that precipitated my PTSD but that it not how life goes. Today I'm happy, and critically I'm not afraid. If I'm honest, PTSD has redefined me, I am a more patient person these days and okay with feeling low, anxious, and even a tad scared when there are reasons to be so. But negative thoughts no longer dominate my world, and I am free of the nightmares and depression.

I did not get to this place of safety under my own steam. Neither did I manage to produce this book without help. A big thank you goes to my dear friends, Seren Phillips who persuaded me to publish my scribbles with the funny bits included, Pam Poppe and Rachel Livermore for tirelessly commenting on drafts and book title options. Andy Taylor deserves thanks for keeping me sane whilst generating creative pen names. A special thanks goes to Dave Carey who read my work and caught all the spelling mistakes missed by spell check, the most poignant being sacred instead of scared and neigh instead of nigh. Dawn Robinson, Mel Hill, Rowena Hughes, and Jane Winter for walking and talking as I engineered my way through a divorce and PTSD. I thank the day Gemma Tysoe kindly urged me stop work to seek professional help. I thank Dr Gregory for being a kind, understanding and thoroughly human GP and Hazel Adams, my counsellor, for tact, tissues, and therapy. Gratitude goes to my brother and his wife for providing refuge in the hills of Wales with great G&T's when I needed a break. Finally, I thank my nippers, for their constant support, love, kindness, empathy, company, and guidance. Their belief that I would get through PTSD with time and patience spurred me on.

Thank you for listening!